GRASSMAN

OHIO'S NORTH AMERICAN APE

JOEDY COOK

CONTENTS

Introduction: Grassman-

Ohio's North American Ape

About the Author

Joedy Cook

Is a cryptozoologist and field researcher For the Ohio Center for Bigfoot Studies and the North American Dogman project. He has appeared on the History channel Monster quest , SYFY Sightings & Encounters. Destination America Monsters and mysteries in America. Joedy currently lectures and exhibits at events across the United States.

To contact the Author

oc4bfs@hotmail.com

ACKNOWLEDGEMENTS

Sebastien-Ecosse Cover art

Ron Shchaftner pictures and field report

Douglas Wheatley Artwork

Seth Breedlove Minerva Monster DVD Art

George Clappison

Christopher Murphy

Terry Endres

John Sewuel

Dana Smith

Tony & Loren Greer

Esieban Sarniento

Pete Travers

INTRODUCTION
BAPTISM BY BIGFOOT

In 1993, I was in the army and was stationed at a remote base in Michigan. At one point during my stay there at the base, two officers had reported that they had seen a Bigfoot next to their tent in the woods near where the soldiers would do drills. Reporting the sighting was apparently a bad idea. While there were no official military sanctions taken against them, they took a whole lot of grief for their sighting. They were constantly made fun of and ridiculed for claiming to have seen a Bigfoot. They stuck to their story though, and, despite the ridicule, they never went back on their claim that they had seen a Bigfoot in the woods that day.

When this was all going on, I was somewhat involved in the paranormal field. While at that time I hadn't considered doing any extensive studies of the Bigfoot phenomenon, I was involved with a paranormal group known as ASK, the Association for Scientific Knowledge. Essentially, ASK was a group of ufologists who would spend the majority of their time researching reports of UFOs and other close encounters with aliens.

Two or three days after those officers had seen the Bigfoot in 1993, I was participating in a military exercise at the range nearby. I was in a jeep in a rather wooded area with three other men. We had to run to the ammo supply point as the final part of the exercise. After using a paved road for a little while, we decided that we would turn the jeep off road in an attempt to get to the road we needed. We turned off road and began to descend a small hill into the woods.

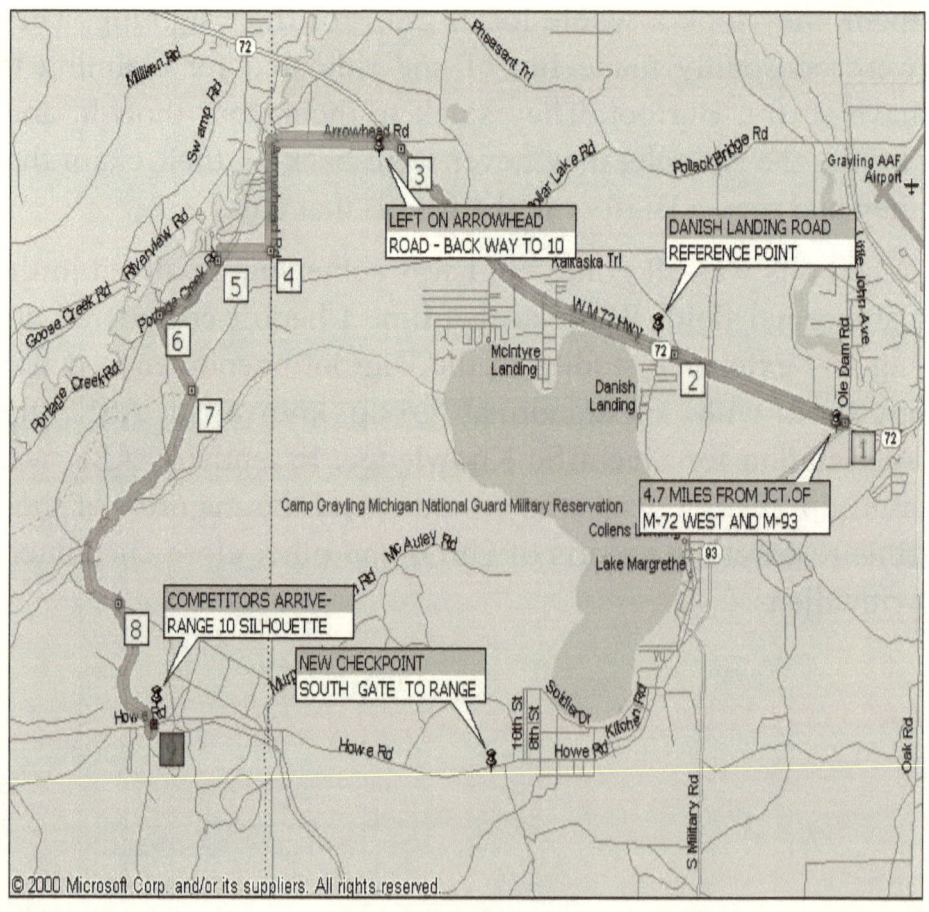

As we proceeded further into the woods, the woods became thicker and thicker. At one point, the woods became so thick that we were forced to stop.

It was summertime there in Michigan so the daylight lasted long into the evening hours. It was probably 8 or 8:30 at that time and the sun was starting to dip below the horizon. While we could still see sunlight in the skies above us, the forest itself was getting to the point where it was somewhat dark.

We stopped there for a minute in the deep woods, trying to figure a way to get through to the road that we knew was ahead of us. Suddenly, something moved in front of the jeep. It was only about 15 feet from us, but it blended into the background almost perfectly. If it hadn't moved, we probably never would have seen it.

It was a Bigfoot. It was a bipedal primate. It stood about 7 feet tall and, from what I could tell, weighed about 500 pounds. Its arms and legs were both very long, and its torso appeared to be disproportionately short. Its hair was a reddish brown color and it was extremely muscular. With every step that it took, I could see its muscles flexing. From my point of view, it appeared to be incredibly powerful; it was built like a linebacker. I also got the impression that it was an older creature. The hair was gone from the top of its head and some of its chest. Other patches of hair were missing throughout its body. Its covering of hair resembled that of a dog with mange.

© Joedy Cook

When it moved, it started calmly walking from our left side to the right. As it passed in front of the jeep, it made eye contact with me. It then just calmly disappeared into the tree-line at our right.

We sat silently in the jeep for what seemed like forever. In reality, it was probably only a minute or two before anyone spoke. Eventually, the driver backed the vehicle up and found his way back to the road.

I was the first to speak. "Did we just see what I think we did?" Everyone agreed. They had all seen the exact same thing. The next point that we had to discuss was whether we were going to say anything about it. We decided that we wouldn't. We had experienced the ridicule that the officers who had reported the Bigfoot received less than a week before. On the one hand, we didn't want to experience that ridicule ourselves. More importantly though, we didn't want to make enemies out of the officers who had reported their own sighting. If we were to report that we saw a Bigfoot this soon after their sighting, it would seem like we were joining in the ridicule of them. It would probably seem to them that our sighting was another jab at them for having reported their sighting.

We agreed to keep our mouths shut about the entire experience and drove the rest of the way to the ammo supply point.

I never told anyone this story, especially being a Bigfoot researcher I felt that this could somehow hurt my own credibility. Now I figure that I'm not going to hide behind what I saw. What I saw was real and it happened. People can believe me, or they don't have to believe me. I have nothing to hide.

At the time I actually saw Bigfoot, I wasn't really that into Bigfoot. I was a UFO researcher at the time. The only reason I got into the study of the Bigfoot phenomenon was that, a year or two after my sighting, our group, ASK, was getting a lot of reports of Bigfoot sightings. We needed someone to move away from the UFO research and start studying Bigfoot. I decided that I would start working with Bigfoot full time.

This book is the result of the research that I have done throughout the last decade and a half. It is my intention to share with you my knowledge about the Bigfoot phenomenon in the state of Ohio. I have included an ecological history of the state, discussions on the ancient history of Bigfoot in Ohio, discussions on the possibility that Ohio could sustain such a creature, as well as many personal investigations that I have done while with the Ohio Bigfoot Research and Study Group and the Ohio Center for Bigfoot Studies.

I hope that this book will not only peak your interest in the subject of Bigfoot in the state of Ohio, but I hope that you will learn a lot and be inspired to begin researching this phenomenon yourselves.

CHAPTER ONE
OHIO'S GEOGRAPHY AND THE OHIO VALLEY

In order to fully understand the Bigfoot phenomena in the state of Ohio, it is important that we first understand the geography and the ecosystem in this environmentally diverse state. Only after we understand the environmental make-up of the state, can we assess whether or not a large mammal can exist here. Further, it is important to understand the geography of the state so that we can accurately assess whether it is possible that a Bigfoot-like creature can remain virtually undetected in the wilderness, and if all of this were shown to be possible, what areas a creature such as this would most likely live.

Ohio itself can be broken down into several different land regions that create an eclectic geography perfect not only for sustaining but also for hiding diverse wildlife. The land regions that comprise the state of Ohio were formed as the result of several glaciers moving down from the north thousands of years ago during the planet's last major ice age. During this time when glaciers would move in and out of what is today Ohio, the state was a very different place. All but the southeast section of the state were completely covered by ice. The glaciers scraped away rock and completely reconstructed the topography of the area. These glaciers produced four well-defined land regions: (1) the Great Lakes Plains, (2) the Till Plains, (3) the Bluegrass Region, and (4) the Appalachian Plateau.

All across the northern border of Ohio, there stretches a region known as the Great Lakes Plains. These plains aren't exclusive to Ohio; in fact, Ohio only encompasses a small percentage of the Great Lakes Plains which stretch all the way from the shores of Lake Superior in Wisconsin to the edge of Ohio in Erie, Pennsylvania. These plains tend to stretch along the banks of all of the Great Lakes. In Ohio, near Cleveland, the plains only stretch ten miles from the shores of Lake Erie. Near Toledo though, the Great Lakes Plain takes up land more than 50 miles from the shore of the lake, all the way through the Maumee Valley, west of Toledo. These plains are lowland areas that are typically quite flat. The soil in these areas are reputed to be quite fertile and therefore are host to a wide variety of flora and fauna.

The Till Plains take up the central and western sections of the state. It falls south of the western parts of the Great Lakes Plains and encompasses the remainder of the largest cities in the state. Columbus, Cincinnati, and Dayton are all situated within the Till Plains. Typically the Till Plains are describes as a gently rolling landscape with a few small hills scattered throughout the region. This is basically true but the Till Plains do contain both the highest and the lowest points in the state. Campbell Hill, in Logan County just south of Lima, is the highest point in the state while the Ohio River near Cincinnati is the lowest point in the state. This region in Ohio contains the most fertile soil in the state and is typically used in present times as farmland. In fact, this section of Ohio is considered the beginning of the Corn Belt which expands westward across the Great Plains and is considered some of the best farmland in the hemisphere.

The Bluegrass Region is the smallest of the land regions which make up the state of Ohio. It juts up slightly from Kentucky in Brown, Adams, and Highland Counties. Its western edge is near the town of Higginsport on the Ohio River in Brown County; its eastern point is near the Appalachia Preserve in Adams County; and it comes to a point, creating a triangular region, near the city of Hillsboro in Highland County. The land here is hillier than it is in the Great Lakes or Till Plains. There is very little flatland in fact. The landscape tends to be constantly rolling or hilly. The soil here is quite thin and is bad for growing crops. It is less fertile than the Great Lakes Plains and the Till Plains, but tends to be more fertile than the southeastern section of the Appalachian Plateau.

The Appalachian Plateau, or Allegheny Plateau as it is sometimes called, is the most topographically and geologically diverse region of the state. It consists of the western edge of the Appalachian Mountains in Ohio and takes up most of the eastern portion of the state. It stretches from about ten miles south of Lake Erie near the Pennsylvania border, all the way down to the Ohio River. Since the glaciers did not traverse the entirety of the state of Ohio during the last Ice Age, the Appalachian Plateau can almost be divided into two regions itself: the section that was covered by glaciers and the section that was not. The northern and western parts of the plateau were covered by glaciers and this section tends to have a landscape that is more fertile and rolling than the southeast two thirds of the region which are rugged with thin, unfertile soil.

are the biggest urban centers on the Appalachian plateau. As a whole though, this region is the most sparsely populated region in the state. The poor farmland and rugged terrain encouraged settlers to move to the more fertile and habitable areas, leaving the Appalachian Plateau as the region with the most undisturbed wilderness.

Since the glaciers formed the Ohio Valley during the last Ice Age, there has been little major change to the geography of Ohio as a whole. As the glaciers began to melt during their latest advance into the area, the melting water created several other features in the state. The water created many caves and valleys as it ran from the glacial edge, down to the Ohio River. The Ohio River itself was largely formed from water melting away from these glaciers about 14,000 years ago.

While many of the caverns in southern Ohio were likely formed by this glacial runoff, Indian legends tell us that some of these tunnel systems are in fact, man-made. There does appear to be some scientific proof to this claim as several ancient tunnels appear to have been carved out with tools, supposedly by the original native people who inhabited this area.

There have been hundreds of sightings of Bigfoot (or the Ohio Grassman—another possible incarnation of Bigfoot in this part of the country) throughout the state of Ohio. The region of the state that holds the majority of sightings of the creature is the Appalachian Plateau in the east and southeast sections of the state. Salt Fork State Park and Shawnee State Park both are situated within the Appalachian Plateau, and these parks are considered by many to be the most active areas for Bigfoot research.

This makes sense since these areas (and the Appalachian Plateau as a whole) are the areas in Ohio that have largely been left alone by civilization. It has essentially remained a wilderness area and not only has the natural habitat of the creature been left undisturbed, but the region has also left vast expanses of woods in which the Grassman can remain hidden from modern science.

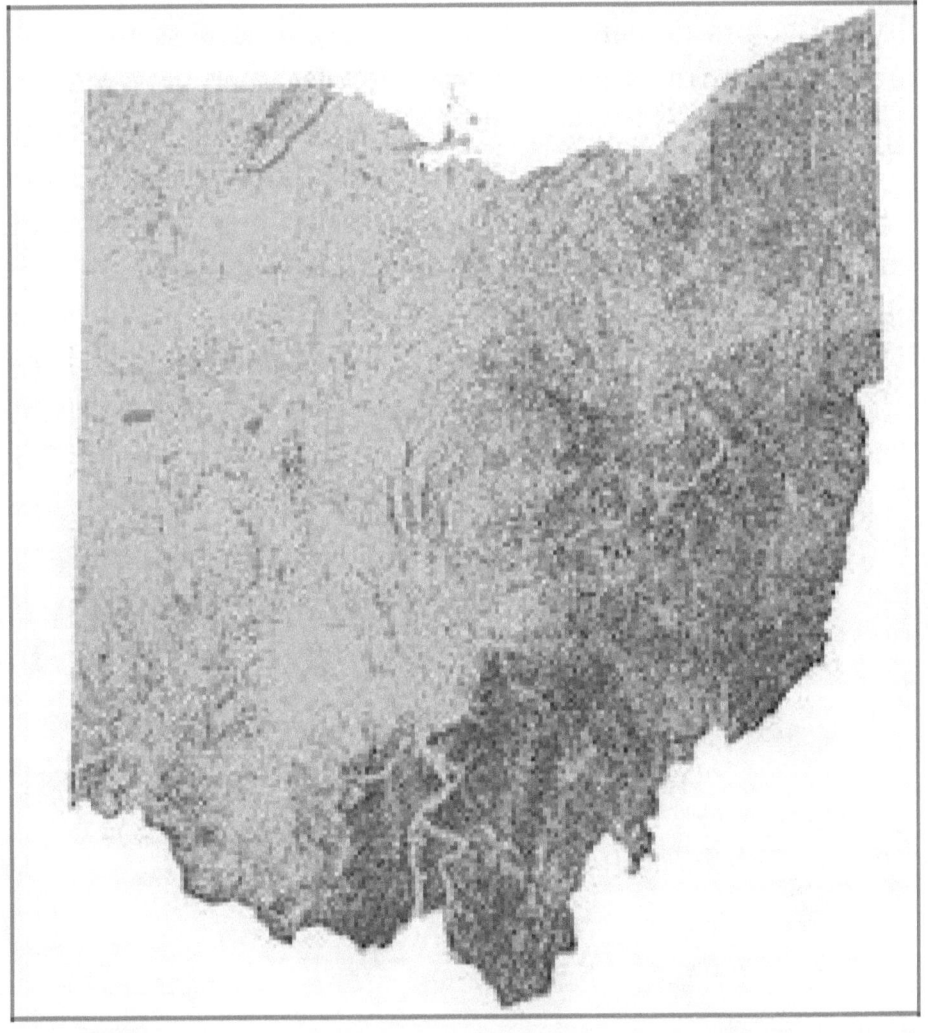

CHAPTER TWO

OHIO'S "BIGFOOT" CREDIBILITY

The first question that presents itself when one thinks about Bigfoot and the state of Ohio is the ability of this state to support a creature of Bigfoot's nature. The creature, as we believe it to be, is a very large mammal that sustains itself entirely on uncultivated vegetation, fish and small mammals. These factors demand vast regions of wilderness that have an abundance of water. Early Bigfoot researchers realized this condition and were quick to point out that the Pacific Northwest was probably the last stronghold for the creature if indeed it did exist. Certainly, the Pacific Northwest has the largest wilderness areas; however, Ohio, together with many other states, still has significant "pockets" of wilderness. Moreover, it is important to note, that of Ohio's 41,000 square miles area, about 81% is rural land or forest areas. The official breakdown (1992) is as follows: Cropland 47%; Forest 24%; Range 10%; Urban 8%; Other 10%; Federal 1%.

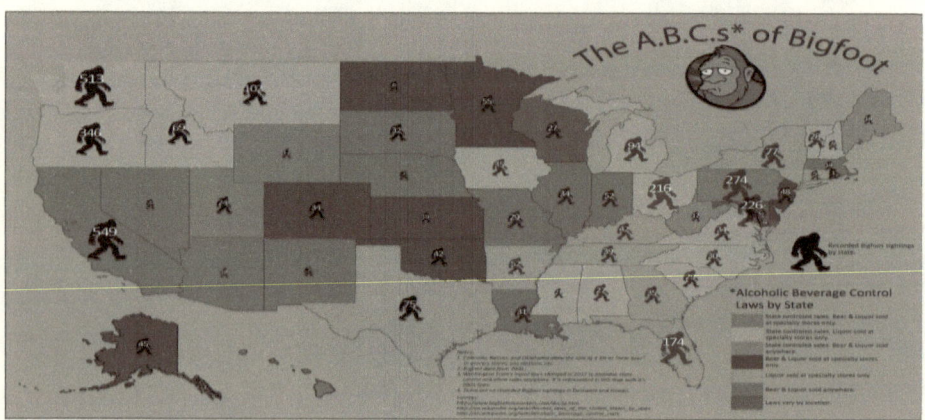

16

When we look at the geography of Ohio, we see that a great water resource, the Ohio River, stretches from southwest Pennsylvania to Paducah, Kentucky where it empties into the Mississippi River. This river, with its numerous tributaries, flows through national forests and state parks with thousands of acres of wilderness and mountainous terrain. Ohio's Wayne National Forest, for example, comprises 108,822 acres. Further, Ohio's 17 state parks comprise over 150,000 acres. In bordering states, there is the Daniel Boone National Forest (Kentucky), with over 670,000 acres, and the Hoosier National Forest (Indiana), with 120,381 acres. These forests, according to the United States Department of the Interior, consist mainly of elm, ash, cottonwood, and pine trees. They are thick, dense forests that support an abundance of wildlife.

The amount of rainfall required to maintain these forests is considerable and, in some areas, parallels that of the Pacific Northwest. Here we might mention that Bigfoot would hold no allegiance to state lines; it would simply move and migrate to areas that could best support its standards of living.

Of all the regions in Ohio, the Ohio Valley in the southern part of the state appears to be the most likely habitat for Bigfoot creatures. We learn that during the Pleistocene Epoch, animals reached great proportions. Driven from their natural habitats by the advance of ice, they proceeded south towards the Ohio Valley. Their craving for salt led many into an area that is now known as Big Bone Lick State Park in Northern Kentucky. This area has many sulfur springs with large salt deposits.

Given these facts, we believe it is highly possible Ohio could support a Bigfoot population.

We certainly do not believe, however, this population would be as large as that in the Pacific Northwest. It is natural that larger wilderness regions would host higher populations. This fact applies to all animals. We can reason to some degree, that the Ohio Valley today would be a highly suitable habitat for a Bigfoot creature. Natural caves would provide protection, and there is an abundance of water together with dense forests for food sources. This is especially true in the central and eastern parts of southern Ohio. Here, the land is remote and is near sources of water such as the Ohio River and many rivers, streams, and creeks which feed it.

Further, these vast areas of wilderness would provide ample space in which these creatures could hide from the encroaching arms of civilization. Few humans have ventured into much of the expansive wooded areas of Ohio. Many deep-forested areas have no man-made trails which cut into them. Beyond this, as was already mentioned, much of this inaccessible wilderness is watered by many creeks and streams. This provides adequate water and therefore food with which to sustain a large omnivorous mammal.

So while the state of Ohio may not be the area that would most readily support a population of Bigfoot-like creatures, it seems highly probable that Ohio could support such a population.

CHAPTER THREE
EARLY OHIO DWELLERS
A POSSIBLE CONNECTION

In order to help solidify claims that there is a population of large bipedal primates inhabiting the wilderness areas of Ohio, we must examine the ways that such a creature may have evolved in this area. To do this we will examine not only prehistoric creatures who were similar in stature and appearance to Bigfoot, but also prehistoric human beings who were also quite tall even by today's standards. Such tall native peoples could have lived in very small populations in the deep wilderness and become completely sheltered from outside influences. Further they could have evolved to look and act like the creatures from Bigfoot stories.

Before we examine the ancient native people who once inhabited the area now known as Ohio, we can mention a possible connection with an extinct Asian primate known as Gigantopithecus. Gigantopithecus was a large primate that definitely lived in China and southeast Asia about 100,000 years ago. The only fossilized remains that have been discovered have been teeth and jaw bones of the creature, but from what they have found, they have determined that it was a very large primate that stood almost ten feel tall.

There is further evidence which could further help to connect this creature with the legendary Bigfoot. Some scientists believe that this creature walked on two legs and not with its knuckles like modern gorillas and chimpanzees. The few jawbones of this creature that have been discovered area all U-shaped and wider at the rear. This allows for the windpipe to actually be within the jaw which means that the head can fit atop a fully erect spine. It shares this characteristic with bipedal humans while knuckle walkers such as gorillas and chimpanzees have a spine which fits more behind its skull. Essentially all sightings of Bigfoot or Grassman report that it walks on two legs and not with its knuckles like most primates.

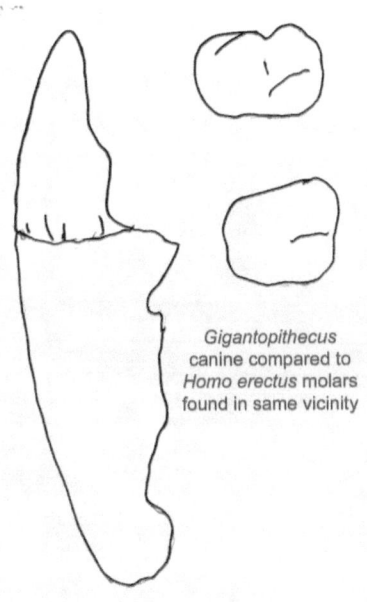

Gigantopithecus canine compared to *Homo erectus* molars found in same vicinity

So what about the fact that Gigantopithecus fossils have   only been discovered in China and southeast Asia? How can anyone claim that the Bigfoot in North America can be a surviving relative of this creature when fossils of this   creature have never been discovered in this hemisphere? The answer to this question is a bit more speculative and depends upon populations and probabilities instead of on scientific proof.

The lack of fossilized remains of the Gigantopithicus in North America could be due entirely to the size of the creature's population in this hemisphere. Every bone of every creature who dies does not eventually fossilize. It takes optimal conditions for a creature's bones to petrify and harden in the perfect way in which to create a fossil. It is very possible that a creature that existed in a certain place amongst small populations of its own kind would never create a fossil in such an area. Since there has never been an actual carcass of a Bigfoot found in modern times, we can infer that if Bigfoot do exist on this continent that they exist in very small populations in remote areas. So the lack of Gigantopithicus fossils in North America does not necessarily mean that there have never been such creatures here.

So if the Gigantopithicus existed in Asia, does that necessarily mean that they spread across the world? The answer to this question is harder to answer and depends more upon speculation than any scientific proof that has yet been discovered. We do know that from about a million years to about 100,000 years ago, Gigantopithicus existed in China. We also know that during this time and earlier, many large mammals from China migrated across the   Bering Land Bridge between Alaska and Siberia into North America. It isn't a big stretch to assume that Gigantopithicus joined this migration of wildlife and some populations of the creature made their way into North America.

So while there is certainly no proof that a race of creatures closely related to Gigantopithicus currently walks through Ohio, the correlation between what witnesses to Bigfoot report to see and what Gigantopithicus may have looked like are uncanny. Further it is entirely possible that Gigantopithicus once roamed the North American continent and may have been able to survive in remote wilderness   areas such as the Pacific Northwest and parts of Ohio.

But extinct giants such as Gigantopithicus isn't the only possible ancient connection that Ohio could have with the Bigfoot phenomena. There are also documented findings of actual ancient humans in Ohio that were quite a bit taller than what we would consider normal. Perhaps these peoples are the link between documented history and the legend of Bigfoot.

In America's pre-historic times, it is said that a band of giants, probably survivors of the Olmed and Toltec civilizations of Mexico, settled for a short time in the Ohio Valley, opening trade routes. Who were these giant people and is it possible they are in some way connected with the Bigfoot phenomenon? This question remains unanswered. However, we can reason that if there were giant native people in North America, they would have had giant ancestors. It may be from this ancestral line that a Bigfoot "native" somehow became isolated or segregated and carried on to the present day.

This line of thinking originated after Sasquatch or Bigfoot creatures were seen in British Columbia, Canada. The Encyclopedia Canadiana states in its entry on "Sasquatch" that: "The finding in 1932 of the remains of a long-extinct race of giants in Mexico gave some impetus to the belief that the remnants of a prehistoric race of troglodytes (i.e., the Sasquatch) may have survived in British Columbia.".

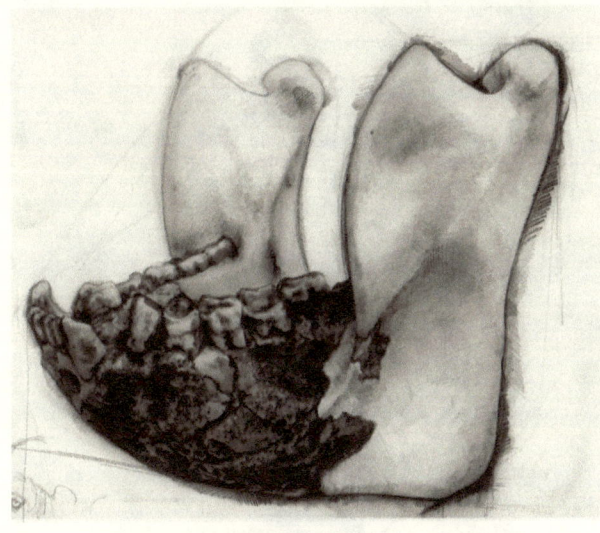

There appears to be some evidence supporting the fact that early "giants" lived in Ohio and its bordering states. There is a story that in 1833, a coal miner in Ohio broke into an ancient tunnel and discovered 17 fossilized human bodies that were very large. Also, twelve-foot-long human skeletons are said to have been found beneath the city of Lexington, Kentucky. Further, in the region surrounding Bowling Green, Ohio, very large human skeletons were found in the Indian mounds in this area. Some of these skeletons were as large as eight feet in length. The Great Serpent Indian Mound in Adams County, Ohio is one-quarter mile in length. It is one of many mounds in this area built by prehistoric Ohio dwellers. One may infer from its immense scale that those who built it were also of immense stature.

It is believed that the earliest known people to settle in Ohio were Archaic men. These highly primitive people are believed to have settled.

there about 5,000 B.C.E. Very little is known about these people. In 1876, two men exploring a cave in Louisville, Kentucky reported that they found a large underground room containing a stone vault. They opened the vault and found three skeletons nearly nine feet in length. Finally, in 1884, Indian mounds were excavated in Christian County, Kentucky that supposedly contained the perfect skeletal remains of an unusually large race of people.

There is also a remarkable giant human skull that was found in Nevada which might also provide some testimony to the existence of these North American giants. This skull, which is much larger than a normal human skull, was found in the Lovelock Cave area. Other bones from this area indicated they belonged to a race of people ranging from 6.5 feet to 10 feet in height. These measurements were based on the skeleton femurs. Many anthropologists disagree with the calculations, stating that the tallest they could justify was 5-feet 11-inches. However, the skull remains a mystery.

Unfortunately, all the hard evidence involved in most of these finds has since been lost to history…or perhaps it is locked away in various museum basements, waiting to be rediscovered. Regardless though, these discoveries have become nothing but stories without the scientific proof required for mainstream recognition of the finds.

On the other side of the coin, there is also possible evidence that Ohio was the home of a race of pygmy natives. Pygmy natives would have been a species of humans which were incredibly small in stature. While directly, a race of pygmies would, on the surface, seem to go against the possibility of a Bigfoot in the state, it does open up the idea that Ohio is in fact an environment which could support a very diverse spread of human-like races and species. So if Ohio in fact was able to support and attract a race of pygmy people, could it not also be reasoned that Ohio could attract and support a larger race of people?

During the last century, Dr. S. P. Hidreth, a professional archaeologist and native of Marietta, Ohio investigated many aboriginal remains in the Ohio Adena mound builder area. This area is located one mile south of the city of Coshocton, on a bluff overlooking the Killbuck River. This area is also found within the Appalachian Plateau, the most biologically diverse and isolated wilderness in the state. In 1853, Hildreth found what might have been a pygmy cemetery. The cemetery had more than three thousand stone-carved graves, each containing a small human skeleton.

skeletons ranged in size from three to four and one-half feet. Processed wood was discovered around the bones, indicating that wooden coffins were used. Archaeologists remain divided in their opinions on this discovery. Many believe the remains were those of children, but others maintain the craniums of the individual skeletons indicate that the bodies were those of human adults.

Cherokee Booger Mask

Perhaps the most convincing ancient historical evidence supporting claims that a large primate roams the forests of North America has to do with documented Native American art depicting ape-like creatures. Many pieces of Native American art, such as totem poles and ceremonial masks and woodcarvings, have detailed carvings of large apes. On the surface, this may not sound strange, but, other than humans and possibly Bigfoot (or Sasquatch as the Native Americans in the Pacific Northwest called the creature), there are no primates that are indigenous to the North American continent. Some of the carvings in question were built by Native tribes which had had no contact with white Europeans who had seen primates. So the question becomes, how did these native people know how to carve an image of a monkey without ever having had the opportunity to see one within their lifetime. A possible answer to this question would be that they had seen such creatures, just as many modern witnesses have seen Bigfoot, a large primate itself. Perhaps these Native Americans had seen Bigfoot themselves and had chosen to carve its likeness into their art.

Opponents to this theory suggest that the Native Americans who created such carvings had indirectly been in contact with a European who had brought a monkey across the Atlantic Ocean. This theory states that perhaps natives on the east coast had seen the monkey, carved the art themselves, and then through trade and contact with these coastal natives, Native Americans from Ohio and further west became familiar with the monkey's image. If this were the case though, it seems strange that these native tribes would choose to use this image of a creature they had never seen so prevalently in their art—especially since these people were known for their reverence towards nature itself. Why would they use images of a creature that they had no proof actually existed in nature— unless, of course, they had actually seen Bigfoot themselves and so therefore had personally seen the image in the wild.

This possibility is probably echoed most clearly in the Delaware First Nations people. These Native Americans primarily inhabited Northern Ohio, and much of their art echoed their fear of the Bigfoot.

They designated a section of their lands as "wildman country" since they were afraid of the wild men who inhabited this section of land. They actually posted carvings of ape-like faces at the entrances to "wildman country" in an attempt to warn fellow members of their nation that they should not tread in that land. The sign towered ten feet above the ground, warning all not to cross into that dangerous wilderness. These native people also had a special weapon with which to kill the beast, a short ax with a stone blade and a wooden handle. While many anthropologists believe that these stories are simply myths that rung true within the Delaware Nation, it is certainly possible that these myths began with a grain of truth.

© TRAVERS
THEPAINTEDCAVE.COM

So throughout the history of the region which would become Ohio, many different splinters of evidence have surfaced both suggesting that an 8 to 10 foot tall primate could have evolved here, and even evidence that suggests that such a creature as Bigfoot could have existed here and interacted with the Native Americans who lived here hundreds of years ago.

© TRAVERS
THEPAINTEDCAVE.COM

Cherokee Booger

CHAPTER FOUR

BOSJESMAN: OHIO'S FIRST BIGFOOT

Old Lebanon Road runs from just south of Sharonville, Ohio to an area north of Waynesville, Ohio. Sharonville is about 18 miles north of the Ohio River and is part of the greater Cincinnati area. Originally, the area was part of a vast wilderness and was inhabited in large part by the Shawnee. In 1787, John Cleves Symmes, a lawyer and politician from New Jersey and member of the Continental Congress, made a land purchase in the area known as the Symmes Purchase. Vast expanses of land were included in this purchase. The western border of his land was the Great Miami River; the eastern border was the Little Miami River; the southern border was the Ohio River; and the northern expanse of this purchase expanded all the way up into Butler and Warren counties

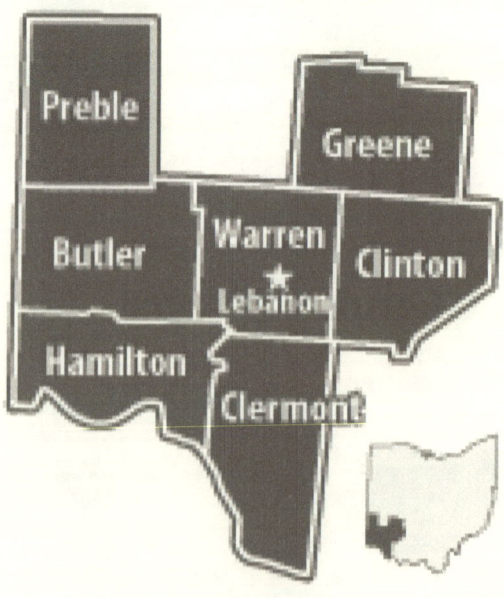

Symmes began selling off his land to settlers in the late 1700s and cities and towns began to pop up all around his land. The biggest city was called Losantiville, a city which would eventually change its name to Cincinnati, but there were many other smaller towns that made up his original purchase. In this chapter, we will discuss perhaps the first Bigfoot to ever interact with European settlers in Ohio, and then we will examine reports of continued Bigfoot activity in the same area. This first sighting and many other sightings throughout the years have occurred within the Symmes Purchase along Old Lebanon Road. The town that is primarily involved in these sightings is Sharonville while many other towns throughout Hamilton County and Warren County have had sightings through the years.

Cave Art of two Bosjesmen's in South Africa

We will begin our story in the town of Waynesville, Ohio. Waynesville was founded in 1797 by an Englishman named Samuel Heighway. The town was cut into an existing forest on the side of a hill overlooking the Little Miami River in what is today Warren County. Originally, the town was quite small, just a few cabins and a tavern. More importantly to this story though, Waynesville was originally almost completely surrounded by dense and undisturbed forest. During the first decade of its existence though, it grew Phenomally quickly as many pioneer settlers moved into the area.

On April 29, 1836, a man named William Henry Venable was born just three miles southwest of Waynesville. When he was quite young, probably around six years of age, William moved southwest to an area near Springboro. As a child, William was very anxious to learn and would eventually turn his life towards the pursuit of knowledge. Despite his eventual move into the academic field, in his earlier years William learned a lot about nature and about the woods. This was common among many pioneers in Ohio at this time since nature was such an integral part of their existence. It was important to know how to hunt and to know how to survive in the wilderness. Essentially, the Waynesville area was still a wilderness. It was just a small pocket of humanity within a vast natural wilderness.

William Venable would become a teacher in 1854, then eventually go to college and become a college professor and author. He was one of the most popular and important writers of his time. He wrote many books and poems about life in Ohio during Ohio's early years.

In Venable's final book, entitled A Buckeye Boyhood that he wrote in 1911, he mentions something very strange. A Buckeye Boyhood is written as a work of fiction. He uses a character by the name of Tip as his main character and tells the story more or less from Tip's point of view. While on the surface, this work seems like a work of fiction, much of the experiences that affect Tip throughout the novel are based on actual experiences from William Venable's boyhood. He takes many of his actual experiences as a boy growing up in the wilderness of a pioneer's Ohio, and he puts them into the novel.

This being said, that the work is actually somewhat of an autobiography based on actual events from early Ohio, the book could contain the earliest account of encounters with Bigfoot in Ohio. The book takes place in Ohio in the time that William Venable was just a young boy.

Since he was born in 1836, we can assume that the book takes place sometime in the 1840s. It talks a lot about living life on a farm during this time and focuses on the simplicity of life at the time and on 'Tip's' love and connection with nature.

Concerning nature, there is an interesting passage involving the things in nature that are cause for fear:

"And there were even worse things to be encountered in the woods than ravenous beasts and fanged serpents, so these inventors of marvels "calculated," with solemn shakes of the head. Tip heard a graybeard farmer tell, with serious air and bated breath, that a "Bosjesman" had been seen clambering and crouching among the branches of a shell-bark hickory in the loneliest part of the swamp-woods on the road to Utica. What a "Bosjesman" might be or do, no one could tell, but Tip conjectured that in all probability it was something between a gorilla and Sinbad's Old Man of the Mountain, and that it was particularly fond of the taste of cowardly blood."

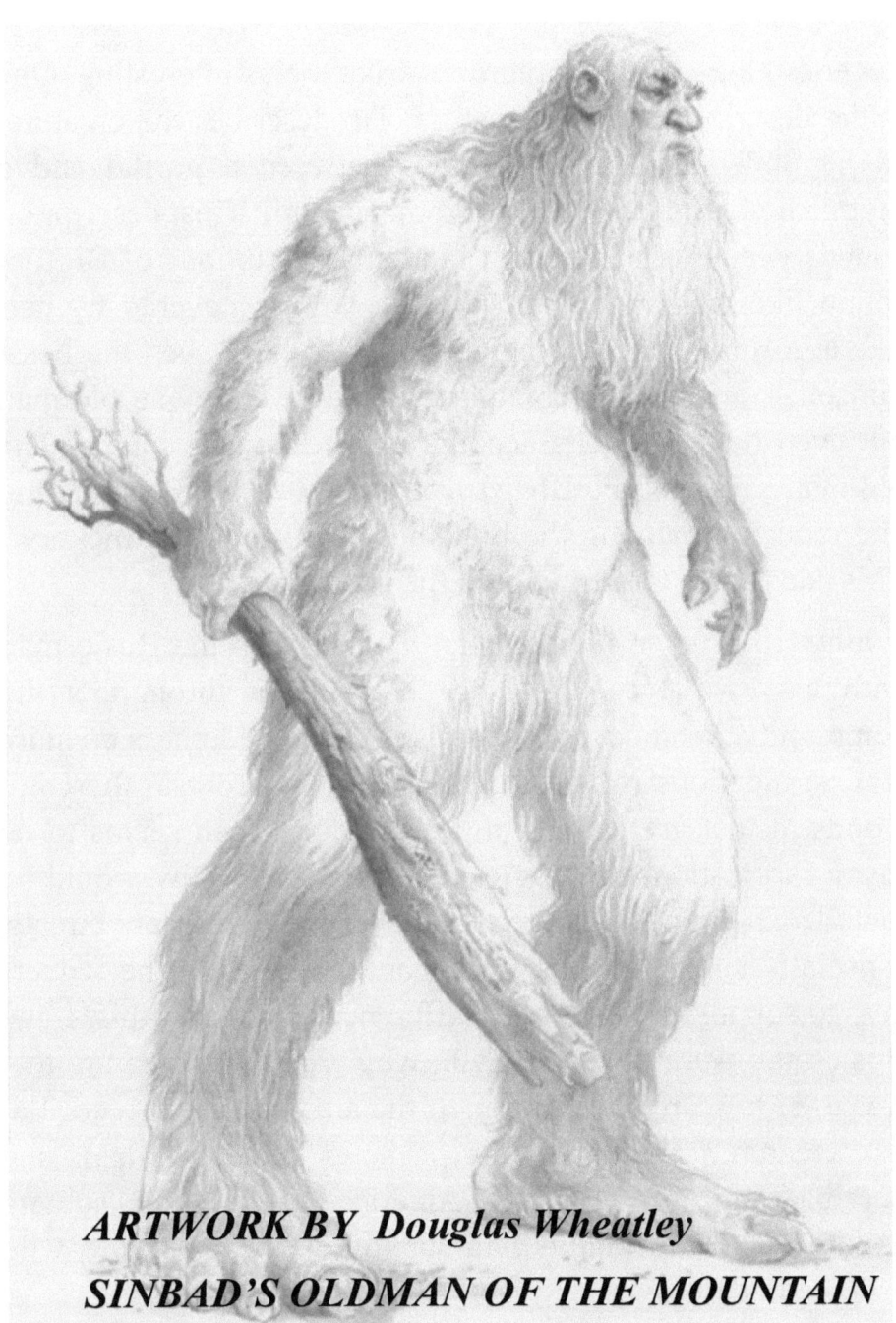

ARTWORK BY Douglas Wheatley

SINBAD'S OLDMAN OF THE MOUNTAIN

Several things in this paragraph strike me as interesting. One is the description of the creature. Tip describes the creature, as he understood it, as a cross between a gorilla and a mythical man from the story of Sinbad. This description sounds very much like what modern descriptions of Bigfoot sound like—a larger than life man who is covered by hair like a gorilla. Next, Tip never claims to have seen the beast himself, stories of the creature are told to Tip by an old man but even the old man's account is a secondary source. The old man says that the Bosjesman "has been seen clambering and crouching among the branches of a shell-bark hickory." This adds some authenticity to the account.

While Tip or even the old man has not seen the Bosjesman with his own eyes, the story is apparent throughout the community. While every other dangerous wilderness creature that he mentions is a real creature that was out in the Ohio woods in that area at that time, the Bosjesman seems to be just a fabrication—a boogieman if you will. Why would he include a mythical creature with these real wilderness threats, especially since Tip was experienced enough in the wilderness to supposedly know the difference? On top of this, if the Bosjesman were in fact a myth, why would the creature that was used to scare the children of the area have been a gorilla-like creature? There were no primates (except humans and possibly Bigfoot) in North America at the time, so any children and most adults had supposedly never seen a wild primate in their lives.

adults had supposedly never seen a wild primate in their lives. The only pictures or accounts of primates should have only been through books. So why would the 'monster' of the woods have been a primate instead of something more frightening and real? A logical answer to this question would be that people in the area were in fact seeing a large primate in the woods of Warren County in the 1840s, or someone had seen an actual Bosjesman in the woods at one point and the story had grown out of this encounter.

Next, we will examine the name that the old man gave to the creature in the woods: Bosjesman. Translated from Dutch or Afrikaans, Bosjesman refers to "man of the bush." "Bosjes" is genitive of the word for bush, spelled "bos" in Afrikaans. Variations of the spelling, "Boschjesman," and "Boskopman." "Boskopman," refer to a late Pleistocene southern African man who is an ancestor of the modern Bushmen or Hottentots. Also called boskopoid, "bosko" means bush and "oid" indicates a similarity or likeness. Boskopoid then would mean "like a bushman." So the name itself seems to imply that it is describing a man who lives in the forest off of nature itself.

Next, the sighting location is in the swamp-woods on the road to Utica. This is important because many of the sightings of Bigfoot in Ohio has referenced him living in the woods, often times near swampy areas. Since the 'mythical' beast from the story is also seen in the swampy wilderness areas of southern Ohio, this is an important correlation to more modern Bigfoot reports from more widespread reaches of Ohio.

The road to Utica is a reference what is today Old Lebanon Road which stretches down to Sharonville and up near Waynesville. In deciding whether the stories related by Venable are just myths or if they have any correlation to modern Bigfoot sightings in Ohio, we will examine some more modern sightings in the area where the Bosjesman was said to haunt in Venable's book.

In the spring of 1931, strange things began happening in the wilderness near Sharonville, Ohio. Sharonville, on the "road to Utica" that was referenced by Tip in the book, is directly adjacent to a large wilderness area. It is known as Sharon Woods and is today still a pocket of wilderness surrounded by development. It was made into a Hamilton County Park, so much of the natural wilderness has been left undisturbed in the area. In 1931, Sharonville was quite a bit smaller than it is today. Eisenhower hadn't yet instituted the Interstate Highway System, so it took a little longer to drive out to this area from the large metropolis of Cincinnati. The old Lebanon highway, the "road to Utica" as it were, was the major traffic artery that went through Sharonville at the time.

In the spring of 1931, people in the area started hearing strange noises emanating from the wilderness which would become Sharon Woods. The noises were a loud, eerie howling, which would always occur at night. It was different from any sounds that anyone in the area had heard before. Many of the people from Sharonville at the time were quite familiar with nature, and they were sure that the howling was not from any creature that was known to inhabit those woods.

Several posses were organized to find whatever creature was making the sounds. Armed men with dogs would for several days go into the forest searching fruitlessly for whatever it was that was making the sounds.

One boy was awakened one night at 3 a.m. by his mother. She woke him so that he could listen to the strange sounds himself. He described the sounds as sounding like an exhaust whistle on an old truck or the high pitched shrill of a steam locomotive. Later in life, the boy would become a woodsman himself and become quite familiar with the sounds of nature. Throughout most of the remainder of his life, he never heard another sound anything like the sound that he heard that one night when he was a boy.

This all changed one day when he was listening to the radio. He was listening to a nationally syndicated talk radio show that was discussing the Bigfoot phenomenon in North America. During this radio show, they played a tape of what the host claimed was the howl of a Bigfoot. The man from Sharonville immediately recognized the sound as the same sound he had heard that night in the spring of 1931.

The area around Sharonville would be host to several other sightings of strange Bigfoot-like creatures over the next 70 years. In 1995, in nearby Madisonville, Ohio, a sighting of Bigfoot was reported, but no hard evidence of the creature was recovered from the scene. Later, in 1996, in the town of Norwood, ten miles south of Sharonville, police followed up on reports of a strange creature.

Law enforcement officials originally described the creature as a bear, but then surprisingly changed their description, saying that it was instead a dog running on two legs. Surprised citizens called the police when they sighted this creature, all of which reported that the creature was running on two legs. Neither dogs nor bears run on their hind legs, so perhaps this creature was something else entirely.

Another sighting happened in Sharonville during 1985 and 1986. A woman related this story to George Clappison and Roger Olson. The woman was only a teenager at the time of the sightings. The teenage girl had no knowledge at the time of the history of strange monster sightings in the Sharonville area.

There was a small wooded area near Sharonville in which the girl and her friends would often 'hang out.' The nearby neighborhood was built on hillsides with adjacent drainage basin areas into which several small creeks drain. This drainage basin area is surrounded on all sides by parking lots, backyards, and residential streets. The water, which flows through the area and into Sharon Woods, will flow through large drainage pipes that will often times go underneath these residential streets and parking lots. The drainpipes in general are about 50 feet long and are about four or five feet in diameter.

The first time the girl (who for the purposes of this description we will give the pseudonym of 'Jane') saw the creature, she was with a friend named Karen and several others. They were hiking in this wilderness area and had found their way down to a creek. They had not been to this particular creek before, so they descended to the banks of the creek and approached one of the long drainage pipes where the creek ran underneath the road.

It was the middle of the day, so the sun was shining brightly enough to illuminate the tunnel itself. The light was clearly visible at the other end of the tunnel, and everything within the tunnel was visible as well. Jane saw what looked like a pile of sticks and debris sitting about halfway through the tunnel. She took notice of this pile of debris since something about it did not look quite right. It was very large, and she did not understand why it was all up against one side of the tunnel wall. It was also arranged in what appeared to be an impossible configuration. It did not seem possible for the sticks or whatever it was to all be stacked up as they were.

Jane decided that she was going to take a closer look and approached the entrance of the tunnel to peer inside. Karen walked up beside her to look. Suddenly, the pile of debris stood up, proving that it was not a pile of sticks at all but a creature. The creature stood on two legs and was completely covered by long shaggy hair. The hair on its arms hung down a full foot and the rest of the hair on its body swung back and forth as it moved. It saw Jane and Karen, turned, and ran away very quickly.

This sighting was not the only one in which Jane was involved. Several months later, Jane was again near the same woods with a group of friends. They were sitting near a small graveyard on the outskirts of town, just hanging out and talking with one another. Whenever any of them would have to use the bathroom, instead of going all the way home they would simply walk out into the woods behind where they were sitting to use the restroom. If it were a female who had to use the restroom, she would go in with a friend, two girls would walk together into the woods.

This night, Jane and another girl went back into the woods to use the bathroom. As they walked into the woods, they were very careful to look around to make sure that no one had allowed them in and that no one could see them. As they were looking around, they happened to glance up into a near-by tree and they saw a huge creature perched up in the higher branches. Jane asked her friend if she could tell what it was, and her friend could not fathom what could be that large and perched up in the tree either. It was about 20 feet away from them and was 10 feet high into the tree itself. It just seemed too big to have climbed up into the tree. They thought that maybe it was a strange formation of branches or a growth on the side of the tree. It was too dark to tell exactly what it was.

Cautiously, they took a step closer to it so that they could examine it further. Then it moved. The girls screamed and ran out of the forest as quickly as they could. From then on, they stayed generally clear of the forest at night.

Both of the creatures that she saw looked very similar. They were each about a foot taller than a normal human being and about twice as wide. It walked on two legs, but the thing that stuck out to her the most about these creatures was their long hair. She had never seen a creature like that with such long hair covering every inch of its body. The hair was dark brown or black, and Jane was never able to see the face of the creature. Whenever she would realize that it was a creature and not just forest debris, it would run. She was only able to see its silhouette. Both sightings were in the same general area as well, probably within a hundred feet of one another. This means that it very possibly could have been the same creature on both occasions.

Jane experienced one more strange event during the years of 1985 and 1986 that could have some correlation to the creature that she had seen. She and her friends had set up a nice little area where they could sit outside at night. They had a table, a couple of chairs, and a couch. All of this was set up on an embankment that led down to a small creek by the edge of the woods. There was one house in the area, but the owners of this house did not seem to mind the setup because it had been there undisturbed for quite some time. Jane figured that if the people who lived in the house wanted the setup gone, they would have gotten rid of the table and chairs sooner.

One morning, Jane and her friends went to the embankment and found that everything had been destroyed. Not only had all of the furniture been thrown down the embankment to the creek, but it had also been completely destroyed. There was significantly more damage done to the furniture than the fall down the embankment could have caused. It seemed as if it were all thrown down the hill and then violently smashed to pieces.

So, the area around Sharonville was again a site of a possible Bigfoot encounter. Many people tend to discount Bigfoot encounters when they come from unlikely geographical locations. Most sightings come from places far away from urban centers that have lots of surrounding wilderness. These sightings are essentially the opposite of this. These sightings are from the Cincinnati area and come from places that are almost completely surrounded by urban development.

We at the Ohio Center for Bigfoot Research feel that it is important to investigate all sightings though, regardless of how unlikely they seem because of geography. It is impossible to come up with a thorough picture of the creature if we are unwilling to follow up on every witness we come across. Of course it is possible that all of these sightings mentioned in this chapter are only hoaxes or some form of misidentification, but if they are not, we have to examine that possibility and add these sightings to any collection that we have of Bigfoot experiences in Ohio.

William Venable felt that the rumors of a gorilla-like creature roaming the woods just north of Cincinnati along Old Lebanon Road were viable enough to put in his book about life in early Ohio. Perhaps we should also accept the possibility that Bigfoot could be lurking just outside urban centers as large as Cincinnati.

CHAPTER FIVE
GRASSMAN AND THE KENMORE STURUCTURE

While up to this point we have suggested probabilities and generalities about the existence of a large bipedal primate in Ohio, in this chapter, we intend to give you, the reader, a more detailed look into the phenomenon of Bigfoot in Ohio. What follows in a detailed case study conducted by the Ohio Bigfoot Research & Study Group, in which they were called out to Akron, Ohio in order to investigate a series of sightings.

This investigation was chosen for this book because it contains some of the most convincing evidence that I have come across in such an investigation. Throughout the course of this investigation, we were able to experience a wide variety of alleged unusual occurrences that seemed to be Bigfoot related.

This investigation also represents the genesis of the term 'Grassman' when referring to Ohio's Bigfoot-like creatures. Before this investigation there was not a single instance where the term 'Grassman' was used in print to describe the creature. The term was only used sporadically among residents of Akron who had actually come in contact with the creature. The term was first used in print in my first book, which I co-authored with George Clappison and Christopher Murphy.

The term didn't really reach the mainstream vernacular until the History Channel aired an episode of the series Monsterquest which was titled "The Ohio Grassman." Now the term 'Grassman' is used interchangeably around Ohio when referencing any Bigfoot activity in the state. Beyond this, the term has spread into Indiana and Maryland to describe their own Bigfoot creatures. While the term has become quite popular in the last couple of years, we had never heard the term before until we approached the town of Kenmore, near Akron, Ohio at the start of this investigation.

The investigation that I am about to relate primarily involves two witnesses who wish, at least within the pages of this publication, to remain anonymous. As a result of this, I have changed the names of the people involved in the sighting to Kent Stow and Singer Stow. At the time of this investigation, Kent was 43 years old. Singer is Kent's son, and at the time of their experiences, they lived in the same house.

THE KENMORE SIGHTINGS:

In 1995, a radio show in Akron, Ohio aired a show in which Bigfoot was a major topic of discussion. The radio show had a prominent Bigfoot researcher as their featured guest, and the discussion turned to possible Bigfoot activity in Ohio and surrounding Midwestern states. Kent Stow heard the radio show as it was airing and tried to call in to the radio station during the show to share his own, ongoing, experiences with the creature. Unfortunately, he was unable to get through to the researcher while the show was running.

When he finally was able to speak to someone about his experiences, all the station could offer him was a form that he could fill out in which he could relate his encounters in detail. After receiving the form, the radio station decided to feature Kent and his son Singer, who had also had experiences of his own, on a later episode of the radio program. The show reached a lot of people in the Akron area, and somehow the form that Kent had filled out eventually reached the Ohio Bigfoot Research & Study Group, the group in which I was currently a part.

After reading the form detailing the sighting, the group decided that it carried sufficient interest to merit further investigation. The Ohio Bigfoot Research & Study Group decided that we would become involved in the case.

On a sunny, unseasonably warm 50-degree day in February of 1995, Terry Endres, George Clappison, and I traveled to Akron, Ohio in order to meet and speak with Kent and Singer Stow. As we approached their house, we noticed that there had recently been some snowfall in the area. Small patches of snow remained on the ground, and the soil was still frozen in those areas that had avoided the day's sunshine.

The Stows lived in the Fairlawn suburb or Akron, and the team rolled up to the small white house just after noon. We introduced ourselves and talked to the Stows for a little while. We decided that we would travel to the actual location of the sightings so that he could relate his stories to us while we were actually viewing the location in which the sightings occurred.

We loaded our gear into Kent's van and proceeded to drive out to the town of Kenmore, which was about an hour from the Stows' house in Fairlawn. Kenmore, a suburb of Akron, is where Kent had grown up and had had his encounters with the beast. He directed us to an area between Manchester Road and Main Street and proceeded to tell us the story of his and his son's encounters with the Grassman.

Kent said that there had been stories since he was a boy about unusual creatures in the Kenmore area. Kent and his friends had first seen the strange creature when he was about 13 years old. Kent and his friends tended to spend a lot of their time outdoors, in the wooded areas around town. They would often camp and fish out in the wilderness. Many times, though, while they were out in the woods, they would hear and see strange things. Most often, what they would hear would be some large creature crashing through the woods or splashing around in the swamp near them. Several times, the boys found unusual three-toed tracks which they attributed to the same creature that they often heard moving through the wilderness.

Kent grew up in the area and continued to camp and fish there up until he was an adult. When Singer was finally old enough to join his father out on his adventures in the woods, he came along and became familiar with the terrain as his father was. Dent told Singer about his encounters with the creature, and some of Kent's adult friends reported to them that they were having run-ins with the unusual creature.

Eventually, Singer began to go out into the woods without his father there. Singer would go out with his own friends. One day, Singer and his friends went out fishing at night. They went deep into the woods and stopped on a wooden bridge to check their equipment and to scope the area for the best spot to start fishing. The sun had just dipped below the horizon so it was quite dark by this time. They were standing in a circle on the bridge facing each other when suddenly what Singer described as a "large dark hand" emerged from the darkness and rested on the shoulder of the boy who was carrying the fishing poles.

The boys panicked. They knew that there was no one else on the bridge with them, and they could see the massive size of the dark hand that had grabbed the boy's shoulder.

They all ran away as fast as they could, not bothering to carry their fishing supplies with them as they fled. They cautiously returned to the scene the next morning once the sun had come up and they could clearly see their surroundings. The gear was all lying on the bridge exactly as they had left it the night before. They examined the bridge itself more closely. At the point where they were all standing at the time of the encounter the night before, the bridge was roughly eight feet from the ground below. It would have taken a massive creature to reach the boys shoulder from the ground below the bridge. Upon hearing this story, we suspected that it was more likely the result of overactive imaginations.

A much more believable incident happened to Singer several years after his initial run in with the creature. In 1988, the family had not yet moved to Fairlawn and was still living at their house in Kenmore. One day, Singer decided to go out into the woods alone. He was exploring an area where a cavern had formed somewhat recently. The cave was created by construction debris which had been repeatedly dumped in the area over the past few years. The entrance to the tunnel was smooth, which Singer thought was somewhat unusual having seen several other similar tunnels throughout the woods. As he approached the cave, a large rock, about the size of a softball, thudded down into the dirt near his knee. According to Singer, it seemed as if the rock had been thrown at him. The rock seemed to drop straight down and did not roll when it hit the ground.

Singer immediately left the area, fearful that whatever was throwing the rocks at him would continue to do so. He didn't want to imagine what would have happened if a rock had actually hit him. He ran home and told his father what had happened, and together, they returned to the scene to see if they could determine what had happened. As they approached the area, another rock fell near their feet. As they looked around for the source of the stone, a third rock fell even closer to them.

By this time, it had started to get dark, and it was getting quite difficult to see anything. They figured that it would be in their best interest to retreat from the scene. They hastily departed, but more rocks continued to fall near them. The rocks continued to fall until they cut out of the woods and into their neighbor's yard on their way home.

During their interviews, both Kent and Singer referred to the creature as the Grassman. They said that from what interactions they have had with the creature, it seemed to them that it was playful. Although they couldn't give us any clear details as to what the creature looked like, they both claimed to have glimpsed what they believed was the creature.

THE FIELD INVESTIGATION:

After hearing their stories, we began to investigate the site. The site that was frequented most often and supposedly yielded the most encounters with the creature consisted of a cleared area and a wooded lot. This area adjoined a large section of forest. Most of the encounters actually took place In the wooded lot area of the site. The wooded lot is bordered by the Ohio Canal on the east side and a junkyard on the west side. At one point, part of the wooded lot had been swampland, but that area had since been drained.

The cleared area which led up to the wooded lot was completely littered with debris. Apparently, over the last decade, the area had been used extensively as a dumping ground for road construction waste and for other commercial debris. Piles of bricks, large slabs of concrete, old gas tanks with their ends cut off, poles of rotten lumber and an assortment of other junk littered the area.

The wooded lot in which we were going to base our investigation was private property. Singer told us that the land belonged to the owner of the adjacent junkyard, but he promised us that it wouldn't be a problem. Singer knew the owner well, and he was sure that the owner would not object to our group investigating on his land.

This wooded area did not seem nearly large enough to support a creature of Bigfoot's size. Perhaps an area of this size could support a large mammal for part of the year, but there did not seem to be enough food and water in the area for a creature of Bigfoot's apparent nature to survive there year round. While we immediately had reservations about the possibility of a Bigfoot in the area, we did notice that the wooded lot did provide some passage to a larger forested area. Perhaps the Bigfoot.

would use the small wooded lot for part of the year and then migrate to the larger forest for the remainder of the year.

Even this possibility seemed somewhat unlikely to us. Bigfoot seem to need a large wilderness area that is rather remote or at least separated from humans. Even if the creature was able to use the wooded lot and the larger forest beyond, there is still heavy development surrounding this larger forest in every direction. The Bigfoot would be trapped in this relatively small area that could never support a population of any size.

The only possible way around this fact that we could see is that the creature could make its way to Long Lake, an undeveloped wilderness area to the east of the sightings, if it moved silently at night through a complex network of lightly developed pockets. Once at the lake though, the creature would still be trapped in the forested area on the northeast shore of the lake. If it had tried to migrate any further to the east, it would be stopped by heavy development east of the lake.

Despite these initial reservations about the area, we immediately began a thorough search of the area. We still had some high hopes of encountering a creature since Kent and Singer seemed to have experienced it rather consistently when the lived in the area. Almost immediately, we found some impressions in the melting snow that looked like they could have been footprints which had begun to melt out. The ground underneath the 'prints' was still frozen solid, so we were unable to ascertain from impressions in the ground whether these were in fact unusual footprints and not just some other kind of normal impressions in the snow. Still, we photographed the impressions and continued our search of the area.

Next, we made our way into a field filled with weeds that came up to our waists. As we walked through these weeds, we came across an unusual bed-like structure on the ground. It measured about ten feet long by three feet wide and was completely constructed out of sticks and weeds. The bottom layer was made out of sticks that measured about an inch in diameter. These sticks were piled up about six inches high. A layer of leaves, grass, weeds, and twigs covered this layer of sticks. This 'bed' did not seem like it had been used in quite some time. The state of the foliage that had been used as a covering suggested that the 'bed' had not been used for probably at least a year. This structure was not the first of its kind to have been discovered. On the west coast, many similar structures have been uncovered and the general consensus among Bigfoot researchers is that structures such as these are Bigfoot beds.

The next piece of evidence that we came upon was near an electrical tower which was situated in the area. There were several large bushes near the base of this electrical tower, and these bushes were bent in some places, indicating that some-one or something had disturbed them. The damage to the bushes was such that it would be next to impossible for a small mammal to have done it and difficult for a human to have done it. This suggests that perhaps something larger had somehow messed with those tall bushes.

Next, we came across an unusual print in the mud near the bent bushes and electrical tower. When we first came across this print, it first appeared to us to be a three-toed footprint. It was 10-12 inches long at the ball of the foot.

The heel appeared human since it was narrower than the rest of the print. Upon further analysis of the print though, it began to appear more and more like a handprint rather than a footprint. Eventually the entire team was in agreement, and we concluded that the print was more likely a hand than a foot.

As we moved deep into the wooded area, we came across one of the most unusual structures that we had ever seen erected in a forest setting. We came into a small clearing and in the center of this clearing was a large domed structure that was completely constructed using forest materials from the nearby woods. Upon further investigation, we discovered that the structure was completely hollow. In fact, all three of us could fit inside if we were to sit on the ground. Inside of the dome, there was an unpleasant pungent odor, and we discovered several unusual hairs lying on the ground.

The construction of the dome was not incredibly complex. The frame of the structure seemed to have been made by using larger branches from the surrounding area in order to create a tunnel. This tunnel was covered with smaller branches, and then everything was held tightly together by vines and weeds, which were woven into the branches. Finally, the entire dome was covered by other debris from the forest, and then a top covering of long grass was used as insulation. The dome would work well as a shelter, but a covering of snow would greatly increase the warmth and effectiveness of the structure. Since there was snow on the ground, it is possible that the structure was at one point covered in snow before it had started to melt. The dome in many ways resembled an igloo and could have been used with the same purpose, to insulate against the cold.

We began taking pictures of the structure and actually came across another print, like the one we determined to be a handprint, near the structure. Since many encounters with Bigfoot are accompanied by a pungent smell, we were able to find large handprints nearby, there were unusual hairs in the nest, and there had been sightings in the immediate area, we began to refer to the dome as a 'Bigfoot nest.' We have no solid proof to support this claim since no one has ever seen a Bigfoot inside the nest, but we were later able to discover similar nests in distant areas in Ohio. At least three other nests have been uncovered throughout Ohio, but none of the other structures has been as well defined as this Kenmore structure.

Even more unusual evidence came to light in the area surrounding the nest. Several holes that appeared to have been dug out of the ground were surrounding the structure. Each of the holes were about half a foot wide and a full foot deep. The displaced dirt was piled in the area immediately adjacent to the holes. Again, these holes are another piece of evidence that Bigfoot researchers have in the past associated with Bigfoot creatures. The rationale is that these holes are created when the Bigfoot dig for roots in the ground.

We continued to search the lot and came upon some further possible evidence that a large creature was inhabiting the woods here. Several sumac bushes to the north of the electrical tower were missing their berries on the highest branches. These high branches were somewhere between eight and ten feet above the ground, nearly as high as a basketball hoop. The berries didn't appear to have been plucked off one by one as a bird or squirrel might do, but they appeared to have been 'skinned off.' It seemed as if all the berries on each of these branches had been pulled through some creature's hand or mouth.

Further, these sumac bushes seemed to be evenly spaced from one another. Each one was two to three feet from the one next to it. This spacing is completely natural and is repeated often throughout nature as a result of re-seeding. The strange thing that was apparent here in Kenmore though was that it appeared that one plant in the series had been removed from the ground. At one point, the spot where there should have been a sumac bush had been replaced by a hole, about a foot deep and two feet in diameter. The missing plant was nowhere to be found in the immediate area and there was no excess soil around the hole. It appeared as if someone or something had simply pulled the bush out of the ground manually. Sumac bushes are tight-rooted plants, so removal of the plant without mechanical aid would be highly difficult, if not impossible, especially if done by any species known to inhabit the area.

The last piece of evidence that we were able to collect was also one of the strangest and most compelling. This piece of evidence was not discovered though until after we thought we had finished with the collection of evidence. Throughout the course of the investigation, we had taken many photographs, and after we returned home to process our evidence, we developed the pictures to help us with our assessment. Upon examining one picture, we noticed something that seemed out of place. The photograph itself was taken while we were snapping pictures of the nest. We had decided that we would take photos of the structure from many different angles. I snapped a particular photo of the nest structure with George Clappison standing behind it, which I thought nothing of at the time. Later though, when we examined that particular photo, we noticed something strange in the background.

There seemed to be three figures in the woods at the edge of the clearing that were watching us as we investigated. One of the figures appears to be a woman who was holding, or steadying, a second figure that appears to be a young child. The third figure almost appears to be a bear, or bear-like creature, watching us from close beside the other two. Closer investigation showed that there was even more detail to these figures than this. The child seems to be holding its left hand near its face. Enlarging the photo shows that all of the figures seem to have very distinct facial features, and the fingers on the child's hand can also be distinguished from the background foliage. Since we did not notice these figures at the time the photo was taken, the identity of these figures remains a mystery.

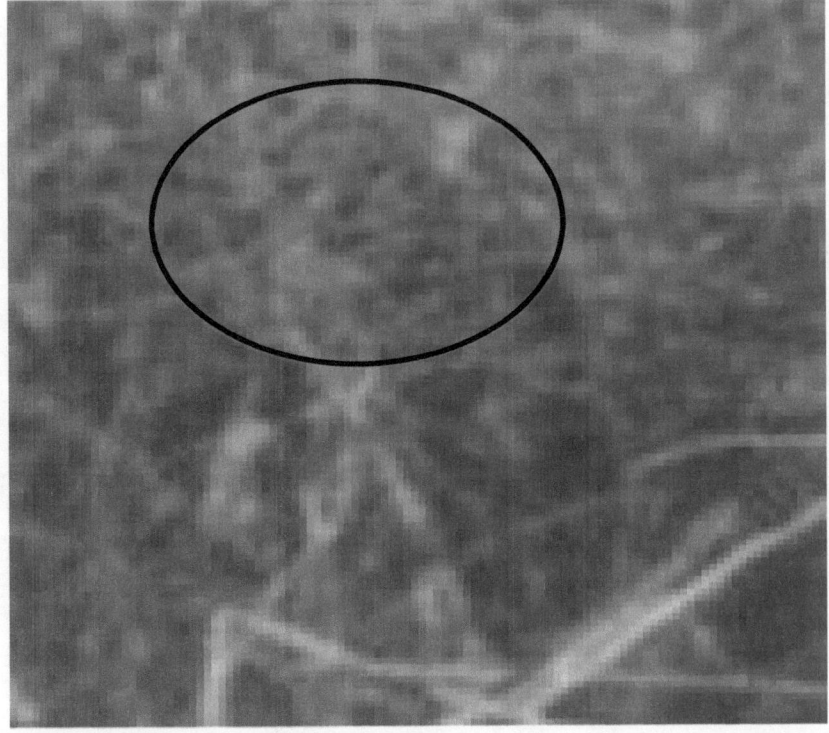

THE ANALYSIS:

Since we came upon a large degree of unusual and intriguing evidence during our investigation of the Kenmore case, we next had to thoroughly analyze what we found. Each piece of evidence was carefully considered and all possible reasons for its existence were examined in this analysis.

Perhaps the most intriguing piece of evidence that we collected during this investigation was that of the Bigfoot nest structure. In the history of Bigfoot research up to this point, many such nests had been discovered and noted throughout the North American continent. Up to this point though, these nest structures had not been closely associated with the Bigfoot phenomenon.

The Kenmore nest is the evidence that most effectively worked to bolster claims that these nests did in fact have some correlation to the Bigfoot phenomenon. Since this investigation, nests of similar structure and appearance have been associated with Bigfoot.

We asked questions about the origins of this nest ourselves and invited other researchers and woodsmen alike to give us their interpretation of the nest structure. In this regard, we received many comments and postulations about the possible origins of this nest. Any explanations that we received short of the possibility that the nest was actually constructed by a Bigfoot seemed to raise more questions then they answered.

One comment that we received is that perhaps the dome is a natural structure, caused by wind or other natural events such as falling branches or storms. In other words, high winds picked up loose forest material and deposited it in a pile. While wind definitely has the capability to deposit debris into neat piles, there are several problems that arise with this hypothesis. First, the composition of the structure itself seems too organized to have been caused by random wind gusts. It consists of larger branches covered with smaller branches and then covered with grass. Wind would not separate the different types of material in such a way. Further, the interior of the structure itself is completely   hollow. It is very unlikely that such a habitable hollow could have been formed simply through debris carried by the wind.

Another possible explanation that we were given towards the origins of the structure was that local children built the structure. While children have definitely been known to create structures in the woods to be used as 'clubhouses' or 'forts,' there are some problems that arise with this hypothesis as well. If children had in fact made this structure, it would account for the intelligence and organization that a structure of this kind would require, but in general this is not the type of structure that children most commonly build. It is too primitive.

Children, most often, will exercise more ingenuity and inventiveness when building structures out in the woods. They will build structures that more closely resemble a lean-to, teepee, or other comparative structure. Further problems with the children explanation involve the quantity and geography of the structures that have been discovered. Nest structures such as this have been discovered in widespread parts of Ohio and across the continent. It is unlikely that children from all parts of the continent have independently come up with the exact same style of building and have, completely separately from one another, built similar structures.

But even if we assume that this is true, that building structures such as these is genetic and that any human child is capable of building a similar 'nest,' then we run into another problem. There has never been a child that has claimed credit for any of the structures that have yet been discovered. Since there are so many of them throughout the country, some in remote areas that children would never be allowed to go by themselves, it is unlikely that, if the children had in fact built these structures, there has not been a single documented case of a child coming forward to claim credit for the dome. Therefore, the biggest problem with the hypothesis that children built the dome structure is that if in fact the structure was actually built by children, someone would have heard about it, and structures such as these would have been disregarded as possible Bigfoot nests.

Next, it has been suggested that the structure is the result of a government bush clearing crew clearing excess foliage from the area. This suggests that perhaps a work crew clearing the area had simply deposited all of the branches and materials in a pile with the intention of returning at a later date to clean up or burn the debris. Again, this explanation runs into many of the same problems as the wind hypothesis. First, a work crew would not deposit the debris in the manner in which it sits at the site. If the dome were caused in this way, the work crew would have had to first deposit the large branches, then the smaller branches, then the weeds and grass. This would be almost the opposite order from what a work crew would actually deposit on the ground.

A work crew would first cut down the foliage and weeds, then would work on the smaller branches. Clearing out the foliage and smaller branches would provide easier access to the larger branches which they would cut down lastly.

If for some reason, the work crew deposited its refuse in the opposite order like it is in the nest, we are still left with further problems. First, the hollow interior of the nest is unlikely to have formed from a random discarding of debris. Even if we allow for the hollow interior, that perhaps the branches were deposited in such a way that a hollow was left inside, there are further problems.

For one, there is only one pile of debris in the area. If there had been a work crew working there, it is unlikely that they would have just used a single pile instead of several smaller piles. Also, as previously mentioned, the nest was on private property. If it were a government clearing crew, they would have no reason to be working on private property. We spoke to the landowner himself and discovered that he was not in the process of clearing his land himself, so the clearing crew could not have been privately hired either.

The final suggestion that we received that guessed at the origin of the nest was that the structure was made by some known animal. There is existing evidence which suggests that raccoons have been known to make nests which are very similar in appearance to this structure. In this regard though, we run into problems with the sheer size of the dome. Raccoon built structures are always quite a bit smaller than this structure. The Kenmore structure is far too big to have been made by a raccoon or even a group of raccoons for that matter. If an animal did in fact construct the dome, it would have had to have been quite large.

There is some evidence that supports the theory that this structure was indeed made by a Bigfoot. A scientist studying primates in California reported to us that African gorillas have been known to construct similar structures in their natural habitats. Since there are no gorillas in North America, it stands to reason that perhaps another large North American primate at a similar evolutionary level to that of a gorilla may be responsible for the structure. Bigfoot, or perhaps Ohio's Grassman (if not the same creature), may well have built this 'nest.'

The next item of evidence worth an in depth analysis is the possible figures which appear in the background of the Bigfoot nest photograph that I took. There appear to be three clear figures watching the investigation unfold, especially when the photograph is enlarged. The first point that needs to be mentioned when examining these figures is the way that they managed to stay unnoticed throughout our investigation of the area. Whatever these three figures were, they somehow managed to stay very still and very quiet while we were there. I did not notice these creatures when I took the photograph, and no one else in our group noticed them either. These figures apparently did not move in the immediate aftermath of my taking of the photograph either. Had anything moved in the brush, one of us certainly would have heard it, and even had we not seen anything, we would have noted that we heard rustling in the brush and associated that rustling with the figures in the photograph. Since there was no sound that came from the woods, had there actually been figures there, they must have stayed and watched us for some time.

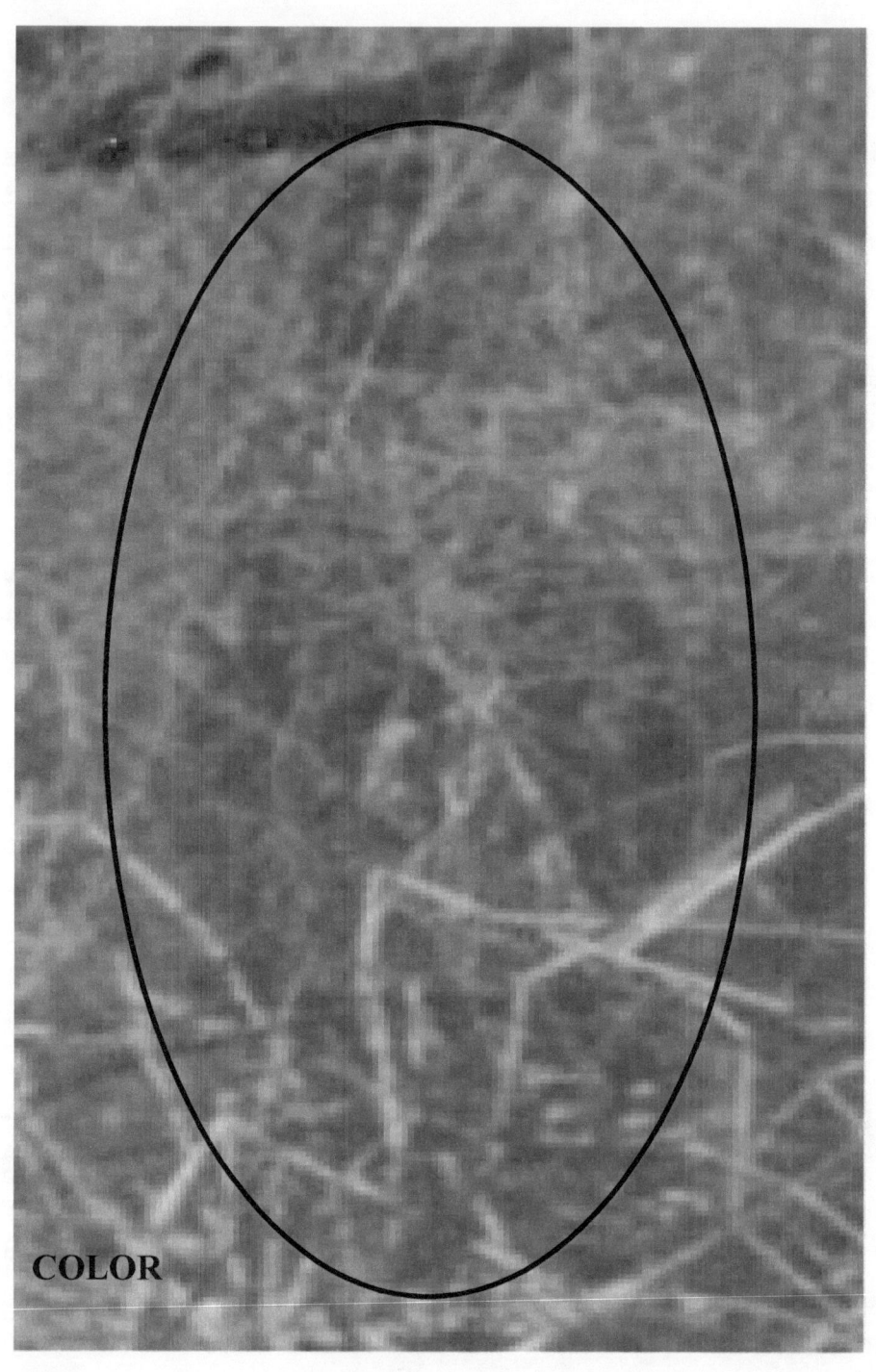

COLOR

The most obvious question that presents itself when examining whether or not this photo actually shows creatures watching us from the woods is whether the figures could have just been the results of shadows and foliage/bush configurations. There are several factors that work to contradict this assumption. The first thing that works to contradict this is explanation is the sheer number of details visible in these creatures. For example, all three figures have facial features when an enlargement is viewed, and all of these facial features are in the correct proportions and in the correct places on their faces. Further, fingers can be seen on the child's hand. The chances of all of this "coming together" in shadows and foliage are very slim—it is possible that something like this occur in one image, perhaps, but in two or three images is incredibly unlikely.

So for the sake of argument, we'll assume that there were actually figures watching us from the woods while we investigated the nest. Who or what were they? Does the fact that they were near the nest necessarily mean that they were somehow associated with it? If they had been some kind of known creature, would they have stayed to curiously watch us? If they had simply been curious human beings watching us, why would they have chosen to remain hidden and unnoticed in the brush? How could they have managed to stay unnoticed in the brush the entire time we were investigating the nest? None of these questions has an easy answer. We do not have sufficient evidence with which to answer these questions.

Had we known that the figures were there the moment that I snapped the picture, we could have investigated further. Unfortunately, we did not have that opportunity, so many of these questions will remain forever unanswered.

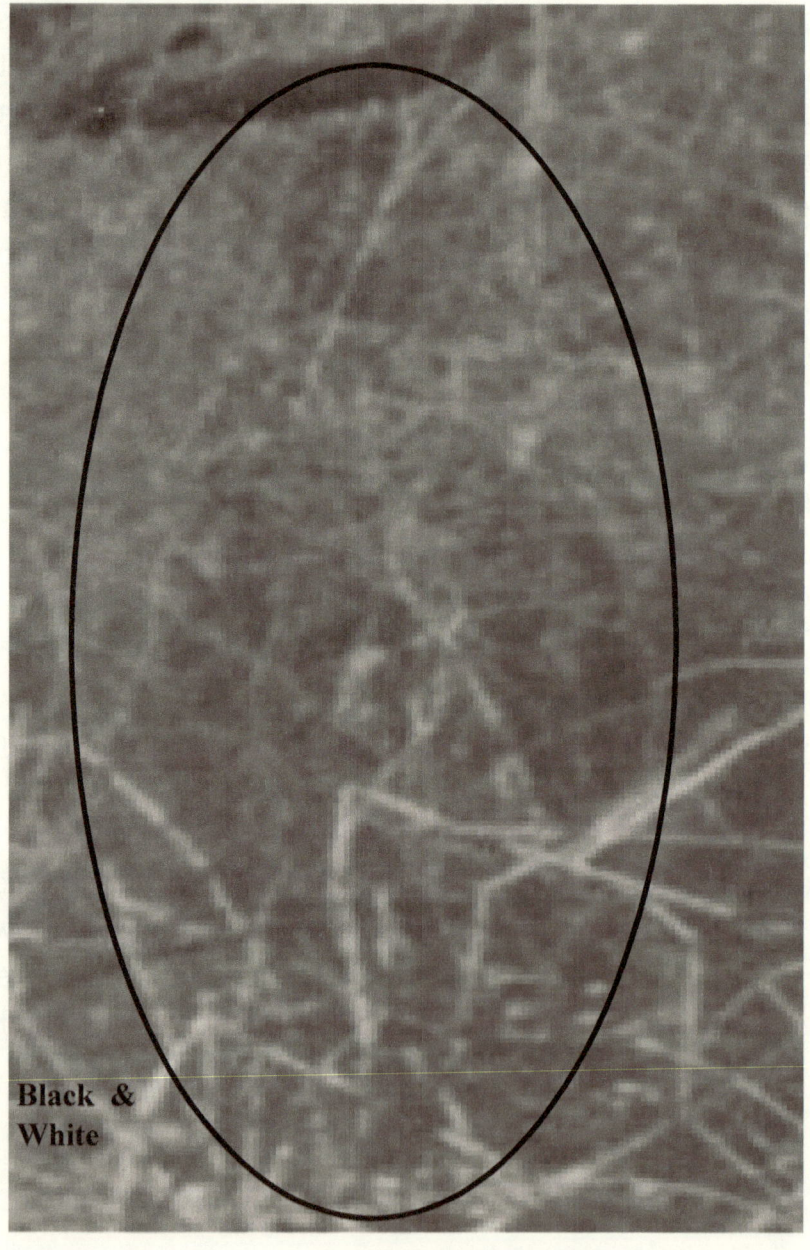

Black & White

Although there is much compelling evidence which seems to be in favor of a possible encounter with a real Bigfoot, there is at least one piece of evidence which seems to argue against the existence of such a creature in Kenmore. That evidence is the problem of the locality of the nest and mysterious figures.

While, throughout the investigation, I tried to rationalize how a Bigfoot creature might wind up in a place such as this, the fact remains that any large mammal the size of a Bigfoot would have a very difficult time not only surviving but also staying relatively hidden in an area such as this. The strongest evidence supporting this fact is that, while the area itself is wild and undeveloped, the area is completely surrounded on all sides by urban development. There is the smaller wooded lot and then a larger connected forest adjacent to this, but beyond this, the woods are essentially completely surrounded by development. The odds of a creature living in this small pocket of wilderness throughout the year and remaining virtually unseen by humans are quite remote.

If a Bigfoot creature were to try to enter this area from remote wilderness or travel from this area to remote wilderness, they would almost certainly be forced to travel through pockets of heavy development. There surely would have been more sightings of the creature if it were to undertake a yearly migration through heavily residential or commercial regions. Further, the wooded area seems too small to support a large mammal throughout the course of the year. A creature of Bigfoot's size and probable appetite would easily starve to death if trapped in this area throughout the course of the year.

So how did it get there? Notwithstanding some "non-natural" explanation or one associated with UFO's, the only answer left is subterranean travel (underground). While we could not locate such a cavern or tunnel that could carry such a creature from this area to a larger wilderness, we are at a loss for any other answer to this particular puzzle.

Another question arises that hurts the possibility of a Bigfoot presence in this case as well. Kent and Singer Stow expressed that this creature exhibited an on-going presence in the area. They would often times, throughout their lives, come into contact with the creature. If this were in fact true, and there was a constant presence of the creature in this area, why have there not been more sightings? Why has the creature not been photographed?

Despite these unanswerable questions, the fact that something, real or imagined, made its presence known in Kenmore resulted in the term Grassman. Kent and Singer Stow used this term exclusively when referencing the creature in the woods. They got the term from other people in the area who had used the term all of their lives. John Sawvel, who lives near the "nest" area, did some investigation for us on the origins of this term. He found a woman who told him that her grandfather once owned property in the area. Her grandfather used the word "Grassman" to frighten children and youths away from his property.

Her grandfather was concerned that local children may set fire to the long grass, which was prevalent throughout the property, and he did not like youths using the property for target practice and outdoor drinking "parties." The woman, who was in her late twenties at the time of this interview, was sure her grandfather coined the term. It is possible that he did, but on the other hand, terms like this often have a source that goes back many years. For example, investigators once interviewed a farmer in the Middletown area who was in his late sixties. The farmer stated that as a boy, nine or ten years old, he recalls his grandfather telling of strangers who frequented that area at the turn of the century hunting for the elusive Grassman.

CONCLUDING COMMENTS:

We have now come full circle on the issue insofar as our current knowledge will allow. Despite some of our evidence that points to the unlikelihood of such a creature inhabiting such an overwhelmingly urban landscape, the nest, the possible footprints and handprint, the unusual figures in the photograph, and a host of unanswered questions are all compelling points which make this one of the more interesting Bigfoot cases in Ohio.

CHAPTER SIX
THE BENTONVILLE CAST

In 2001 I wrote a letter to all 88 county Sheriff departments in Ohio. In the letter I ask if you get any Bigfoot sightings or reports please send them my way. In February of 2002 received a call about a encounter in Bentonville by the Adams county Sheriff's office. The Deputy gave me the contact information of the witnesses. The fallowing day I went to the location of the encounter and met with Dana Smith and Loren Greer. They told me what had accrued on the night of February 23rd. Both of them where at home getting ready for bed when they hard unusual screaming outside their trailer. Dana said that the screaming lasted about five to ten minutes. They both looked out the window and seen what they described as a ''Big Man''. They called the police who investigated the incident but found nothing do to the heavy rain the evening. The fallowing morning Loren Greer's brother Tony scouted the area and found a unusual hand and Foot print next to a ravine by the home. Tony made a plaster cast of the hand impression but was unable to make a cast of the foot print. I was given the hand cast by Tony to do more research on what could of made the impression. I was unable to do a fallow up on the encounter do to my deployment to Iraq. After my tour of duty I tried calling and going back out to the home but unfortunately they have hade already moved away.

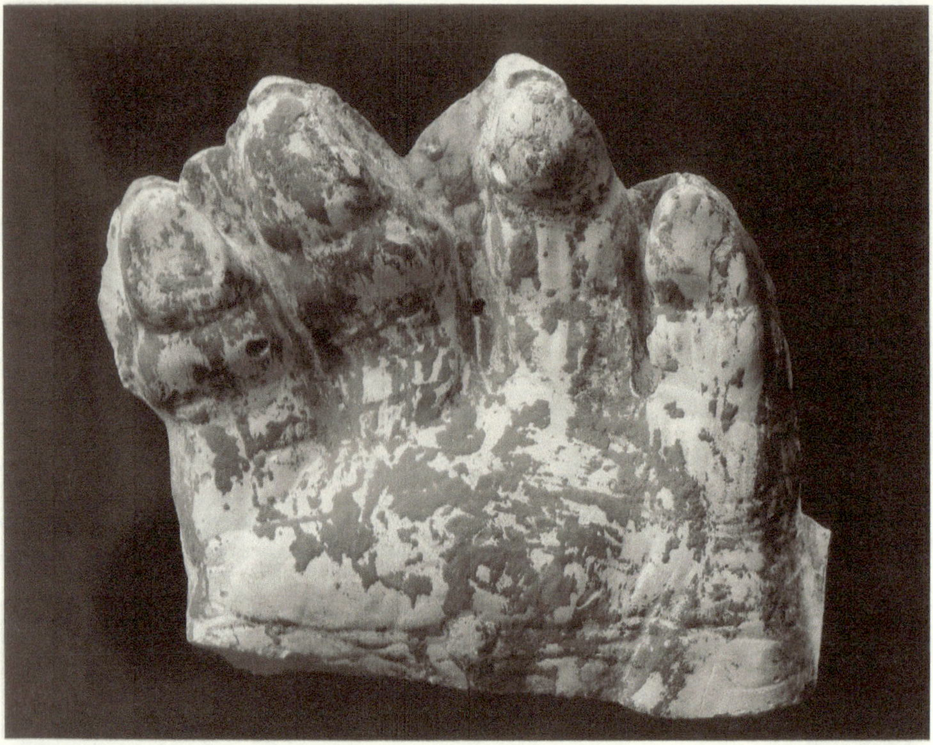

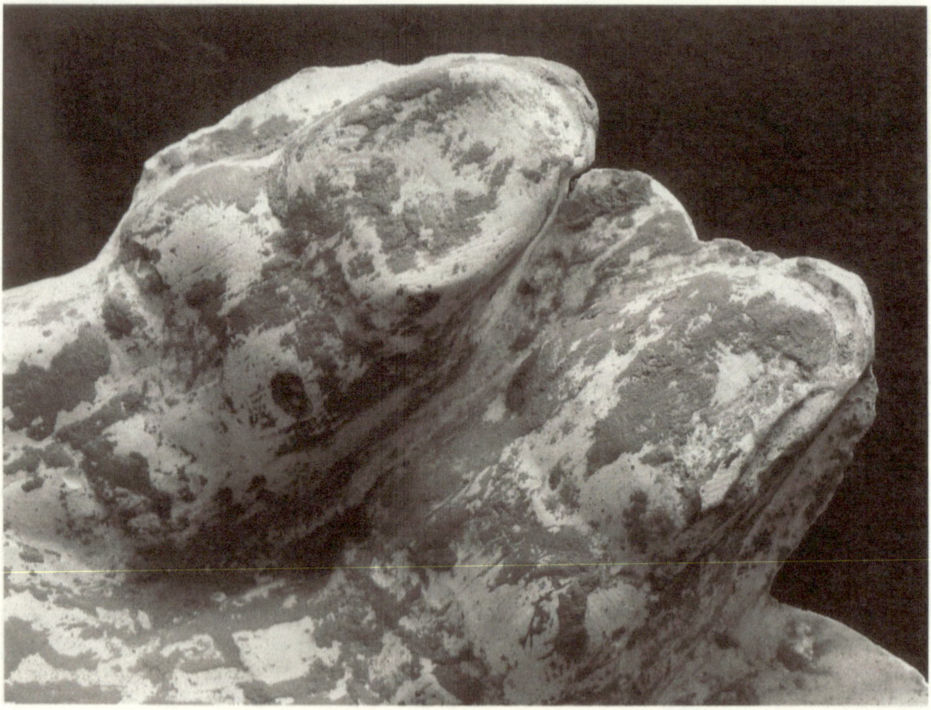

Ohio handcast

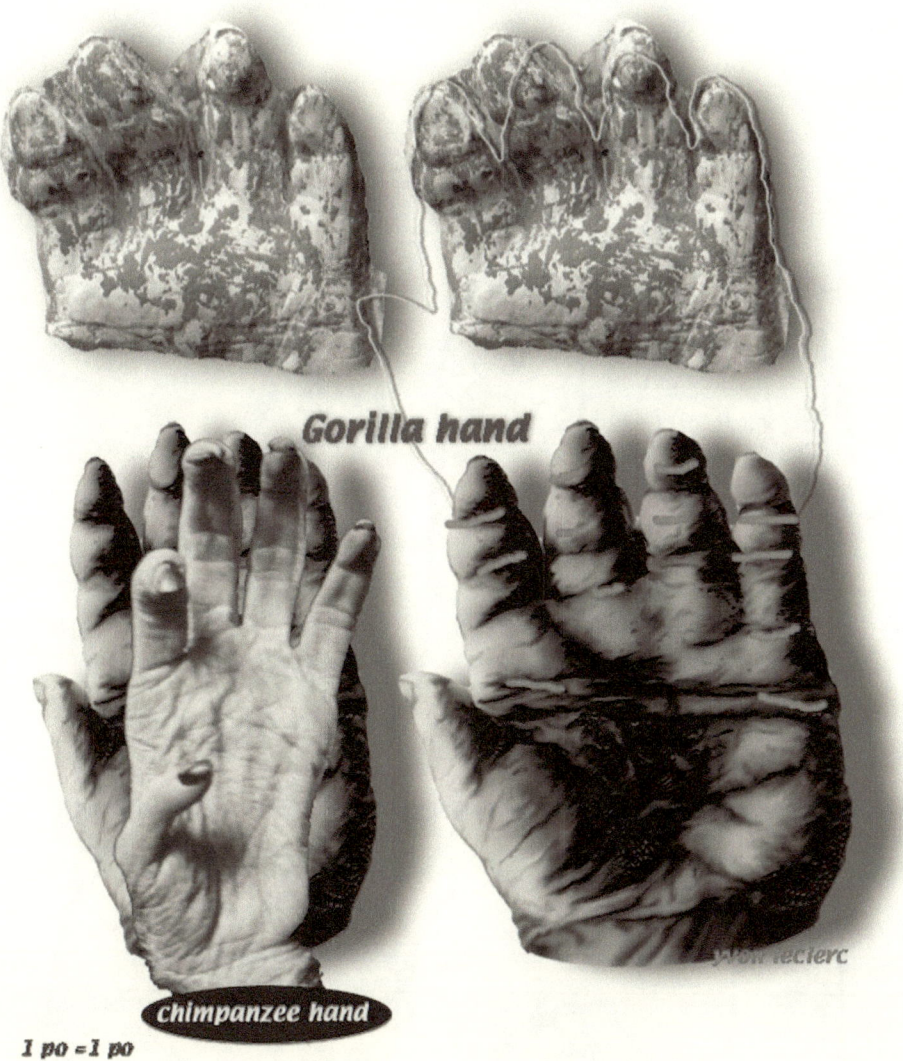

Gorilla hand

chimpanzee hand

1 po = 1 po

Hand cast compared to a
Gorilla and Chimpanzee

DRAWINGS FROM MY FIELD REPORT

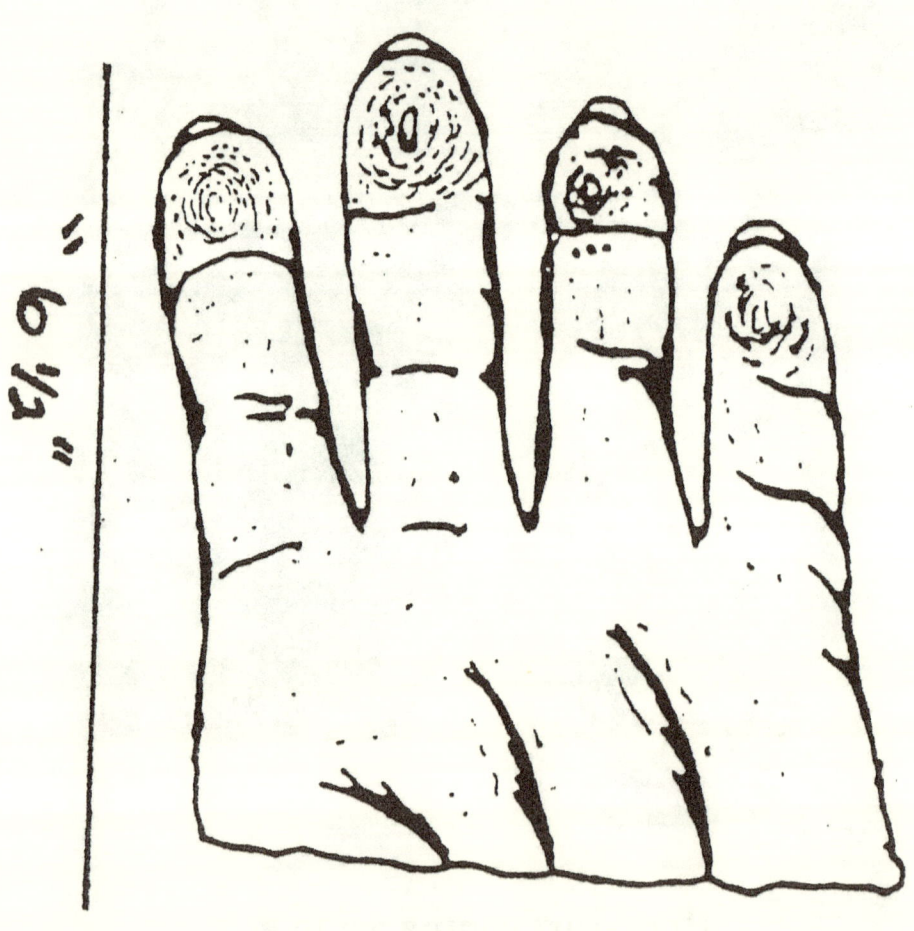

All four fingers has a dermal ridge pattern on the cast.

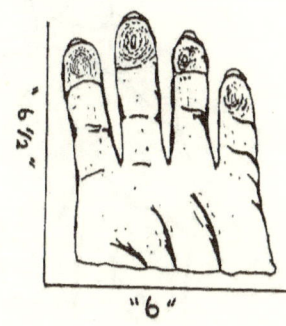

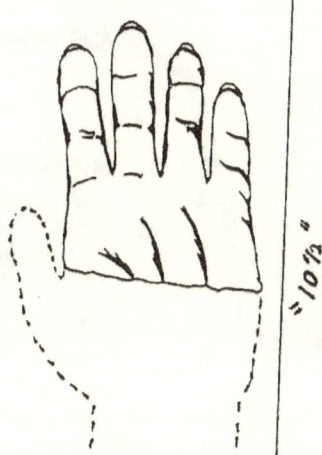

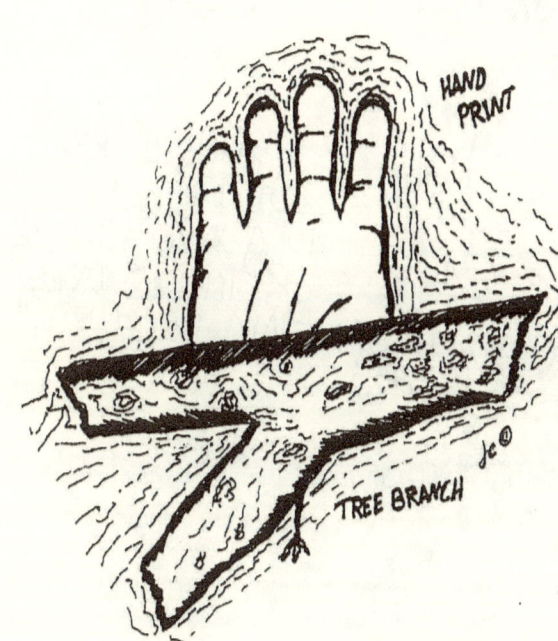

HAND PRINT

TREE BRANCH

Hand Print found on top of Ravine at ohio Brush creek in Adams county ohio by 2 females living in the area.
2/23/02

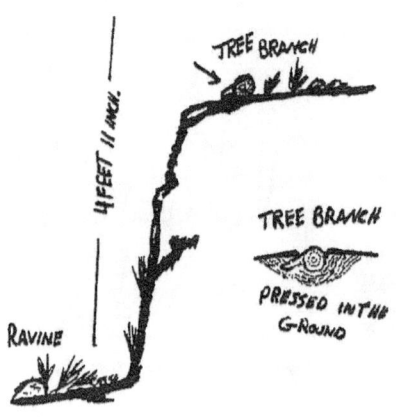

4 FEET 11 INCH.

TREE BRANCH

RAVINE

TREE BRANCH
PRESSED IN THE
GROUND

17"

GRASS

MUD AND GRASS

Imprint of Right foot 17 inches long was found 39 inches away from handprint.

CHAPTER SEVEN
THE TOOTH

In 2013 I was out with friends fossil hunting in the Shawnee state forest. We where walking up and down a dry creek bed looking for Trilobites. I was digging in one area when I found something that looked like a bone. I took my water bottle and washed it off and seen that it was a tooth. The tooth was canine looking but had a grove on it. I took the tooth with me to the 2013 Ohio Bigfoot conference and asked Esteban Sarmiento to look at it. Esteban thought it looked like a primate tooth. He also said it was the lower right canine. I really don't know what to make of the tooth and what type of animal it came from. For the past few years the tooth just set on my shelf. In 2016 I took the tooth to a DNA lab to get tested. The lab stated that the tooth would be damaged in the test do to the condition of the tooth. I did not want the tooth damaged so I'm waiting for a better way to get it tested with out being damaged.

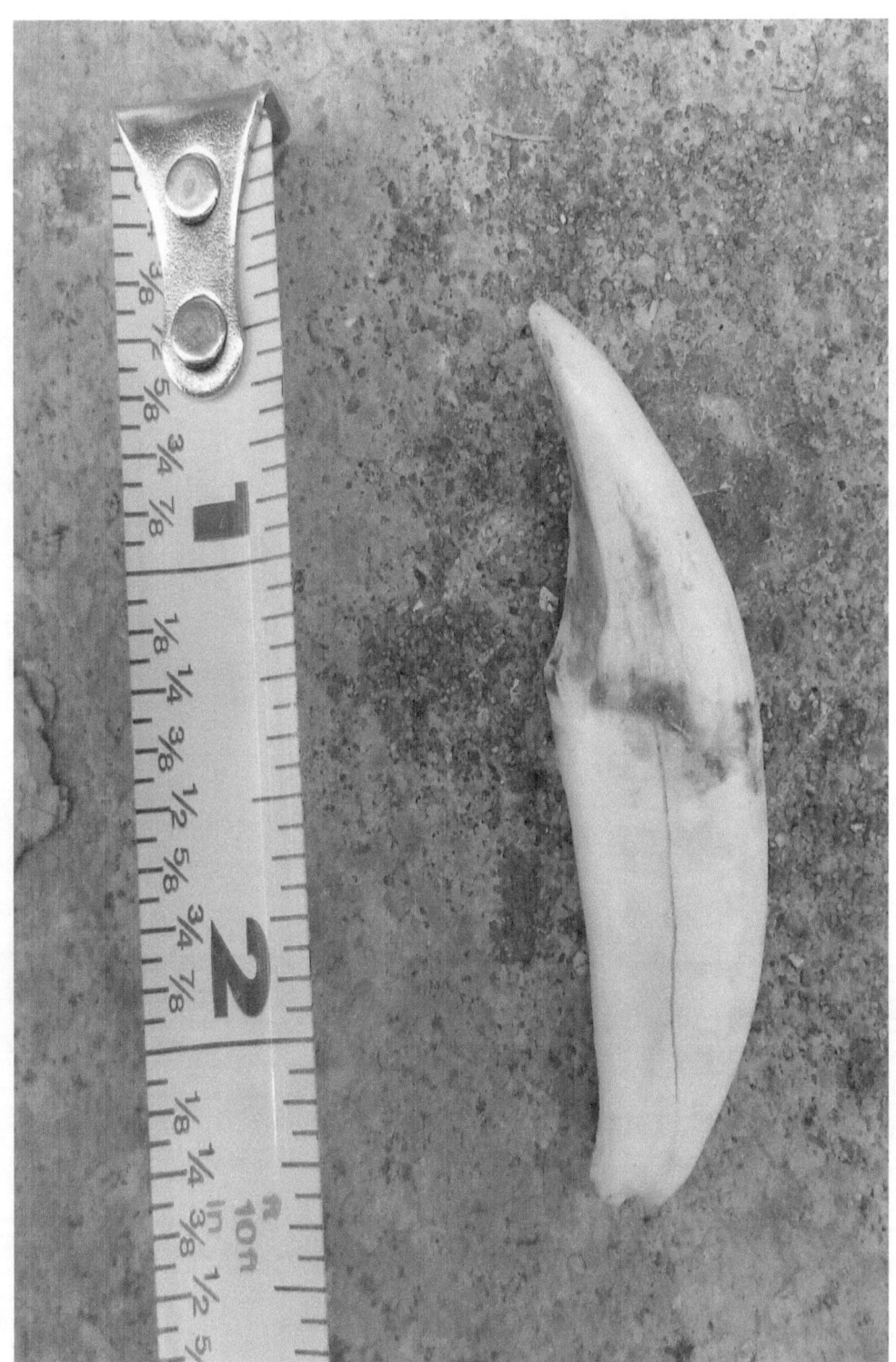

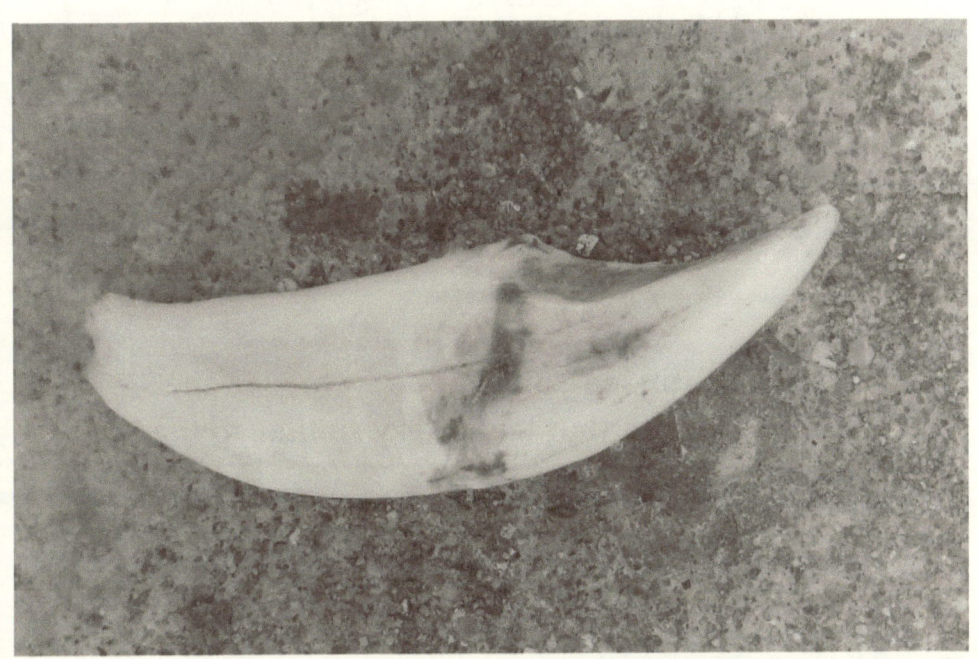

BEAR TOOTH

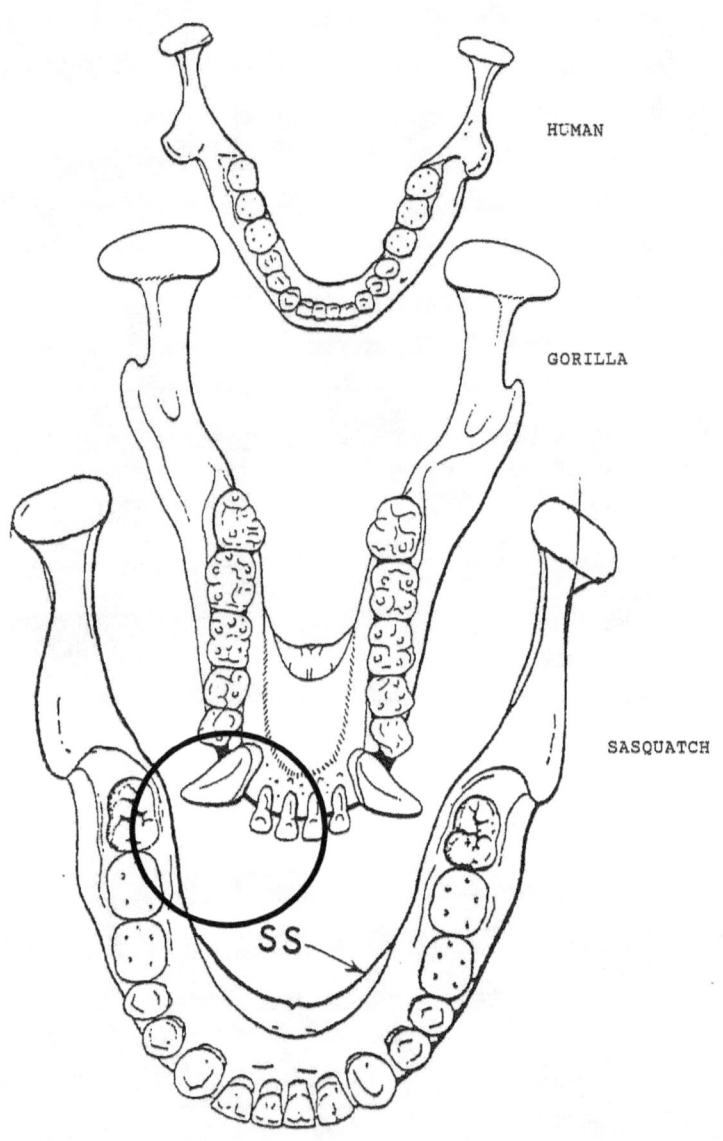

HUMAN

GORILLA

SASQUATCH

S S

43

In this drawing you can see a grove in the Gorilla tooth that looks very similar to the tooth found .

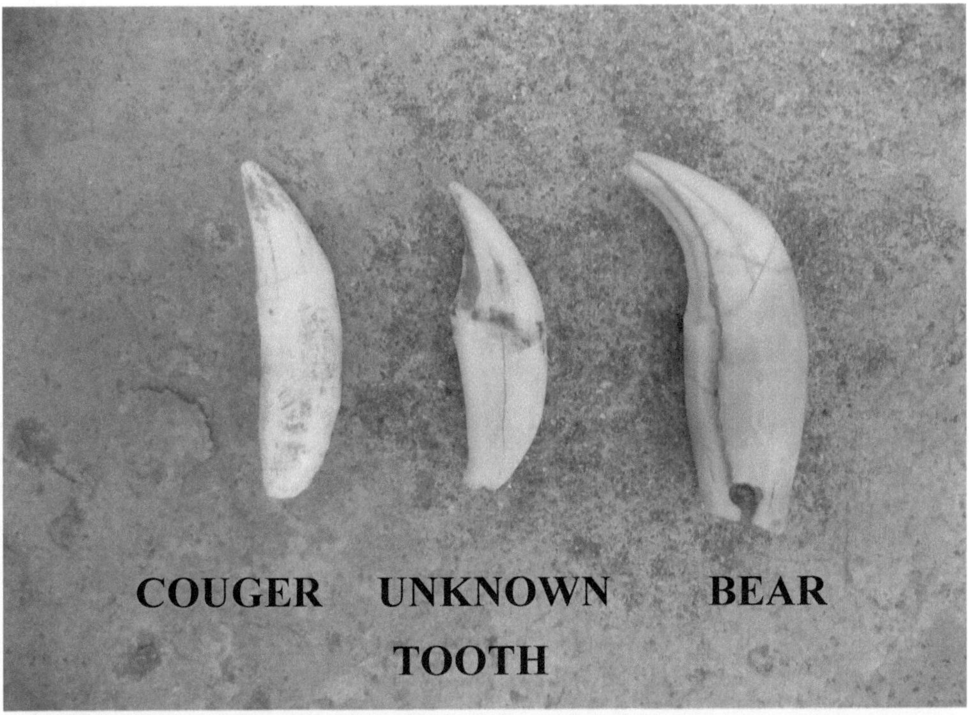

COUGER UNKNOWN BEAR
TOOTH

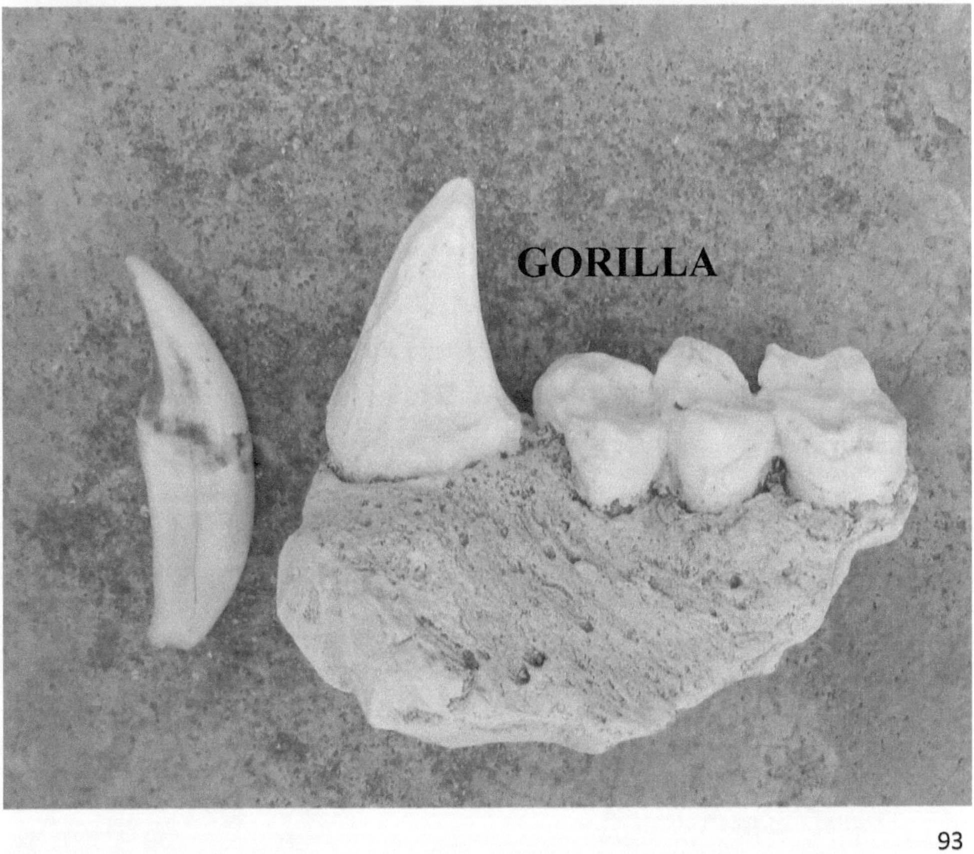

GORILLA

CHAPTER EIGHT
THE MINERVA MONSTER

August 1978

INVESTIGATORS: Ron Schaffner (Ron@bfro.net), Earl Jones, Jim Carnes Jim Rastetter, Iona Boyce, Barbara Mudrak,(Akron Beacon-Journal) and James Shannon (Stark County Deputy Sheriff)

CASE DATA: All of our interviews and field investigations were conducted on the weekends of September 9 and 30, 1978. Other interviews were conducted by the late Jim Rastetter and his research team, the press and local law enforcement. We will list the incidents by date since there are several encounters. There are also many newspaper reports from this time period mostly from the Akron Beacon-Journal. The reader should be aware that these incidents are multiple witness sightings which adds some credence to the reports. The reports of large felines in conjunction with the hominids are a subject that I have never been able to explain.

I will begin with the first major sighting which occurred on 21, August:

Evelyn Cayton's family and friends were out on the front porch when they heard noises in the direction of an old chicken coop just to the right of the house. They saw two pairs of yellow eyes that seemed to be reflecting a porch light. Scott Patterson went to his car and turned the headlights on in hopes of getting a better look. The eyes were emitting from what appeared to be two "cougar-type" felines. Then, the party saw what looked like a large bipedal hairy creature step in front of the large cats as if to protect them. This creature then preceded to lurch towards Patterson's car.

The witnesses fled to the house and called the Stark County Sheriffs Department. While waiting for the deputies, the bipedal creature appeared at the kitchen window - about four yards from the kitchen table. Patterson pointed a .22 caliber pistol at it, while Evelyn Cayton loaded a .22 caliber rifle.

Patterson's 'creature' as described by witnesses to artist Dennis Haas

The creature stood outside the window for close to ten minutes. They all could clearly see the creature because of the back porch light. They decided they would not shot at it unless the creature made any advances toward them. The biped suddenly left without harming anyone. (Sketch of creature is on file with us.)

"It doesn't seem to want to bother anyone", said Mary Ackerman. "It was just curious. We all felt that it wanted to be friends"

Deputy Sheriff James Shannon arrived about 15 minutes after the call was made and about 5 minutes after the creature left the scene. A strong stench was still lingering in the area when Deputy Shannon began to interview the witnesses. Shannon later told reporters that it smelled like "ammonia-sulphur". Extra deputies were brought in and the searched the entire area on horseback and in jeeps. (The land behind the Cayton's was an old abandoned strip mine and beyond that were dense woods going up a gradual hill.) Unusual, but unsubstantiated foot prints were discovered.

22, August:

Mrs. Mary Ackerman, of Minerva drove to the Cayton residence to pick up her daughter and friend. (Mrs. Ackerman is Evelyn Cayton's daughter.) As she turned into the driveway, she saw the same creature standing on top of the hill next to the strip mine. She watched it until it walked out of her view.

23, August: The creature appeared again at Cayton residence. Howe Cayton was not sure if it was the same thing. He fired a gunshot into the air and the figure departed.

8, September:

During the late daylight hours, Mrs. Ackerman observed two "ape-like" animals across the strip mine. She stated that she thought the creatures were standing in a tree but wasn't sure because of the distance. Again, she watched them for a while, until they were no longer visible in the thick weeds.

9, September:

Jim Rastetter interviewed Henry Colt who lives about 5 miles east of Minerva on U.S. 30. He told Jim that he was walking through some woods by his house when he caught a glimpse of an unknown furry animal. Mr. Colt said that the animal was squatting next to a tree and let out a sound similar to a loud cough. Actually, the incidents leading up to the August 21 sighting began about the first of the month. Mrs. Cayton believes the creatures' appearance were due to her husband (Herbert) cutting down the thick brush next to the pit and that he also dumped some garbage around for the raccoons.

Several nights later, Cayton's grandchildren and their friends came running in the house crying in a frightened state. They claimed to have seen a large hairy monster in the pit. Mrs. Keck, Mrs. Cayton and Howe Cayton went outside to see what had scared them. They saw a creature that was covered with dark matted hair. They estimated it to be about 300 pounds and 7 feet tall. "It just stood there", said Mrs. Cayton. "It didn't move, but I almost broke my neck running back down the hill." Mrs. Cayton claims that she later observed the creature in the daylight. It was sitting in the pit picking at the garbage. She could not make out any facial features due to the amount of long hair covering its face. She remembered that the creature had no visible neck.

MORE GROUND LEVEL ACTIVITY AND COMMENTS:

What about the two phantom cougars? This is one of the most puzzling aspects of this case. The "ape-like" creature was described by the witnesses as if to be protecting the big cats. If Patterson's testimony is truthful, the how should we ascertain such statements. Does this mean that these creatures live in harmony with each other, or is it more soft evidence to indicate that all this phenomena is originating from the same source? deputy Shannon said that he received many reports of bear and "panther-like" bobcats in the area. Was the creature a bear? Although the Ohio Division of Wildlife debunked the idea of bears, we know that they are coming into eastern Ohio from Pennsylvania. We also discovered a bear explanation was used by local law enforcement to down play the incidents. This reasoning was used to keep the local vigilantes and hunters away from the woods.

We asked Mrs. Cayton; "Do you think what you saw were bears?" She answered; "No, not unless they were mutated."

Canine Activity: Prior to the August 21 sightings, one of the Cayton's German Shepherds was found dead with a broken neck. The dog had been chained up with a collar to the dog house. The collar was found next to the dead animal still in tacked to the chain. We can speculate that either; 1. The creature jerked the dog out of the collar, or: 2. The canine was so scared that it broke its own neck trying to escape.

Consider the following:

The other shepherd ("Missey") was still in a schizophrenic state during our investigations. At times, she is extremely calm and affectionate and on other occasions, she is scared and vicious. Missey has spent a lot of time digging, which is not uncharacteristic of a canine. However, she dug a tunnel about 8 feet into the ground. This hole is almost large enough to contain two medium sized dogs. Could this be a hiding place for the dog when the creature returns?

EVALUATION:

According to the Cayton's and Mrs. Mudrack, the Sheriff's department did an excellent investigation. However, there are some conflicting reports. The deputies stayed with the family until the early morning hours. They studied alleged prints and hair, but came up with no monster. They covered up the incidents to discourage hunters. They supposedly took the soft evidence to a local college in Canton for analysis. When we tried to obtain this evidence, Mallone College told us they did not receive anything.

Many investigators have since talked to the Cayton family. I believe that they are sincere people who would have no real benefit to hoax. Evelyn had just been released from the hospital due to an ulcer and a thyroid tumor. her doctors told her to avoid emotional stress, so why would she fabricate a story like this? She did not need this type of publicity. One must not forget that this is a multiple witnesses incident. With this many witnesses, (interviewed separately, then as a group) it could be easy for one to "slip up", but all stuck to the same story

One cannot forget about the deputies' investigation and other phenomena surrounding these incidents. The witnesses were unfamiliar with the term "Bigfoot", until the press caught wind of the story. Barbara Mudrack gave us an excellent character reference of the witnesses. She told us (prior to our on-site investigations) that she really believed that the Caytons were telling the truth about their visitor. Earl Jones and Myself visited the Caytons on two separate occasions. On our second visit, we backpacked and spent the night in the upper woods looking for physical evidence. We came up with no evidence, nor did we witness anything unusual. We did feel the need for more hours logged, but were unable to do so, for lack of financial means. (Could not afford lost time from our jobs.)

This case is by far, the most complex and interesting one from my files. (Ron Schaffner)

MAP OF THE AREA WHERE THE SIGHTING TOOK PLACE

REPORT #009
General Map

TO AKRON
I-77
ALLIANCE
o Sebring
U.S. 62
S.R. 183
CANTON
New Franklin
TO I-71 &
MANSFIELD
U.S. 30
STRIP MINES
Boyard/EAST Rochester
LISBON
MASSILLON
Robertsville
E. Canton
MINERVA
Kensington
TO EAST LIVERP
U.S. 30
I-77
S.R. 9
ABANDONED STRIP MINE
U.S. 30
CAYTON RESIDENCE
TO CAMBRIDGE
PARIS TOWNSHIP, OHIO
(RS)

REPORT #009

THE MINERVA CREATURE

DESCRIPTION:

Wt. 300 lbs.
Ht. 7 ft.
Color: Brown
No visible arms.
No facial features
except red eyes that
reflect light.
Strong odor.
Sounds: Cries, grunt.

Copy of original drawing of the bigfoot

Now, nearly 36 years later, the Minerva Monster will be unveiled once again. Featuring in-depth interviews with law enforcement, media personnel and witnesses, Minerva Monster aims to retell the Cayton's story as it never has been before. Against the backdrop of small-town America a myth will become reality. The documentary film is directed by Seth Breedlove, and produced by Jesse Morgan and Alan Megargle with an original score by Brandon Dalo. Minerva Monster is the first in a series of documentaries called Small Town Monsters. Setting aside all the drama, and preamble of previous "monster" documentaries, Minerva Monster will tell the story through witness interviews; the real story, in the words of those who lived it

http://www.smalltownmonsters.com

CHAPTER NINE
EATON OHIO BIGFOOT

Retrospective:

Preble County, Ohio Incident

A Report of an Alleged Unknown Bipedal Animal

and Its Sociological Implications

The field investigator was Ron Schaffner

It was 1977 *"The Year of the Creature".* Historians of the Bigfoot phenomenon will recall this as one of the most active years since the birth of modern day research. Reports were coming in from the west coast across mid America to east of the Appalachian Mountains. A few high profile cases during that time were the result of some outlandish hoaxes, but many submitted reports appeared to be authentic with soft evidence to back up their claims.

The basic scenario was always the same:

People reported large hairy bipedal creatures. Sometimes other people saw a similar creature in the general area around the same time frame. Often times, this generated a flap of reports. Posies were formed and the hunters attempted to track down the creature(s). Sometimes tracks were found. These flaps occurred over several days. But no creature was ever found and bagged. Hunting dogs refused to track the scent. Then, the trail went cold and it is if there wasn't a creature there in the first place.

During April of that year, I had investigated a report in southeastern Indiana, between Aurora and Rising Sun. It was an interesting report involving a young couple that claimed to have seen a large unknown animal at their trailer. The only piece of physical evidence was the dent in his car, which the witness claimed he hit the creature while leaving the scene. Close examination of the automobile indicated no paint or chrome, so we ruled out a wreck. Our investigation of that case was still on going through the next month.

During the third week of May, I was made aware of newspaper accounts coming from the Dayton Daily News about two 13 year old boys claiming they saw a huge, bipedal creature with dirty brown fur that smelled like rotten meat. The report was in the vicinity of Old Camden Pike near the historic Roberts Covered Bride near U.S. 127, just south of Eaton, Ohio. (1)

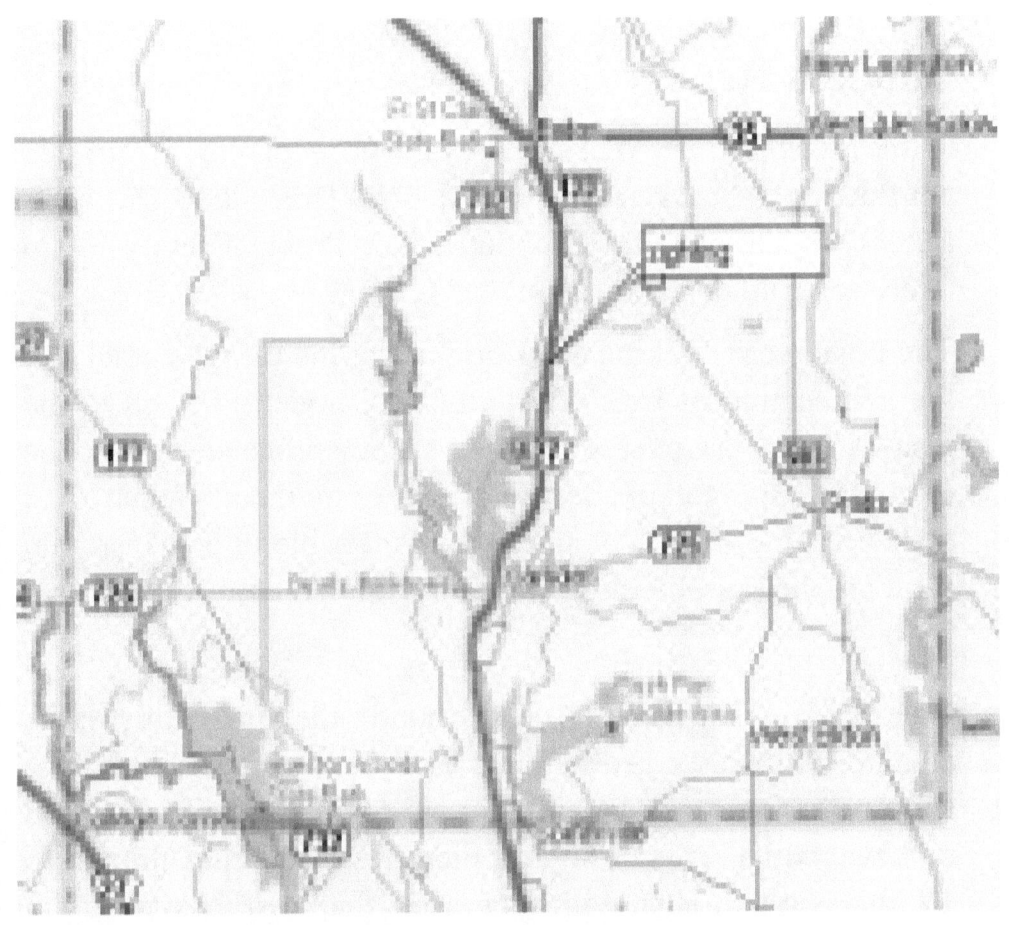

Figure 1: Overall Map of the Region

I contacted the Preble County Sheriff's Department and they gave me the name and address of one of the witnesses. In the meantime, investigator, Betty Parks was granted an interview with the other boy. Betty and I interviewed the boys separately to prevent any possible contamination of their testimony. Since they were minors, we could not mention their names. For the sake of the incident report, we have used their initials.

Incident Report

Witnesses: Two 13-year-old boys whose parents requested confidentiality. Date: May 18, 1977 Time: 8:30 PM EST (DST) Location: Old Camden Pike; Preble County, Ohio (Between Camden and Eaton)

The boys were walking their dog along the railroad tracks to the intersection of U.S. 127 and Old Camden Pike on to the historic Roberts Covered Bridge. As they proceeded along the road, the dog got excited and ran from them. When T.L. picked up the dog, they smelled this terrible odor like rotten meat and heard something walking behind them.

When T.L. and D.B. turned around, they saw this large creature with dirty brown hair. They further described it as about 9 feet tall and weighing about 500 pounds. It appeared to have white eyes. They further described the animal as standing on two legs, with long arms that nearly touched the ground.

T.L. said that it looked like it had black and brown spots on it and its head was rounded with no visible neck.

I was also told that it made a sound similar to a cross between a bird and squealing tires from an automobile.

D.B told Betty Parks that at one point, the creature seemed to be jumping up and down while flapping its arms. He told her that the creature looked similar to an ape.

"It chased us down by the bridge, across a soybean field towards my home. It seemed like it was right behind us, as it took very large steps. When we reached the railroad tracks and the highway, it vanished from our view into some nearby woods." said T.L. in a personal interview.

FIGURE 2 ROBERTS COVERD BRIDGE

When the boys arrived home, they told Mrs. L. what had happened. She immediately notified the Preble County Sheriff's Department and two deputies responded. The boys accompanied the Officers to the scene. They refused to get out of the cruiser while the deputies searched the area. Mrs. L. told us that for the next week, her son would not let any-one open his bedroom window, even though it was hot and humid.

I was impressed with T.L.'s testimony. The boy was really scared during our interview. The description of white eyes seemed odd, so I questioned him very carefully on this matter, but he stuck to his story. Something had frightened him, which he perceived as some kind of "hairy monster."

Meanwhile, investigator, Betty Parks was interviewing the other boy, D.B. at his home with the parents present. He relayed the same story. Betty would later tell me that he showed signs of extreme fright as he recounted the story.

Possible Physical Evidence

A local farmer and a police officer contacted Richard Hoffman in Dayton, Ohio concerning two unusual prints on his property. His farm is located about 1/2 mile northeast of the reported encounter. Hoffman notified us and we went to investigate. Two prints were discovered along Seven Mile Creek. One was in good shape, while the other was severely weathered. We estimated them to be about a week old. They had five toes and measured 14 inches long, by 7 inches wide. The stride was roughly 6 1/2 feet.

FIGURE 3

The print was caste and taken to the home of Charles Wilhelm for further study. We were able to determine that the track showed all indications of normal slippage and mud pushups that are consistent with something walking downwards into a creek bed.

However, we could not find any evidence of a trail due to the amount of foliage on the ground and the hard clay up the slope away from the creek bed.

Unfortunately, there is no evidence to connect this unusual track find to the report given by the two boys. If we allow for witness misinterpretation of the creature's size and weight, this print could be the product of the thing they allegedly saw. There is always the probability that these tracks were the result of a hoax or misinterpretation by a walking human. We could not eliminate that possibility due to the size of the prints and the factoring of weathering.

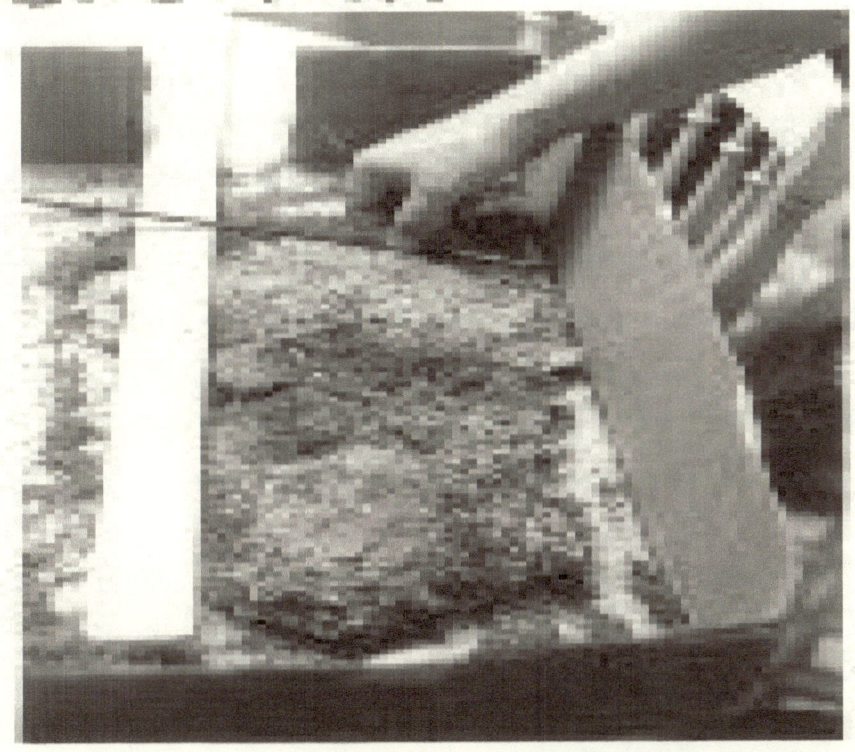

Top

Cast of track found by Ron Schaffner

Bottom

Foot print found under the Bridge

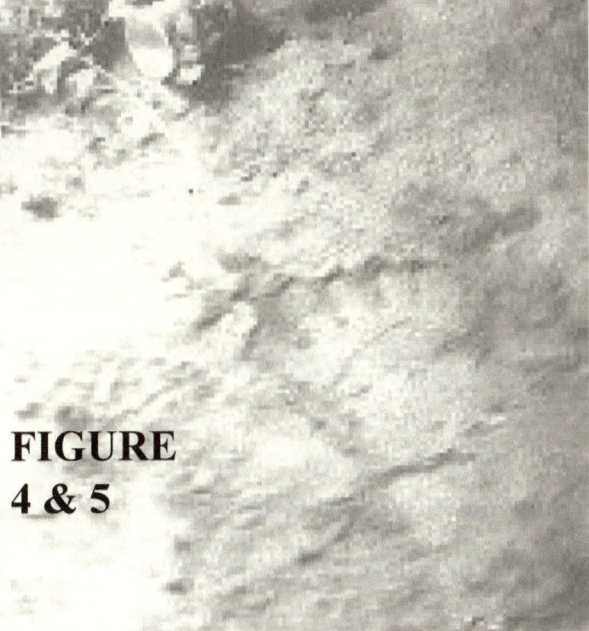

FIGURE 4 & 5

Sociological Impact

As with many Bigfoot reports during 1977, 'monster mania' swept through the county. The 'vigilante factor' was in full swing after the newspapers picked up the story. Suddenly, Preble County and the area of Roberts Bridge became a local hangout for the younger citizens and local hunters who wanted to bag, or at least see this unusual animal.

This year was also noted for the height of the C.B. craze. (Citizen's Band Radio) During our frequent trips to the area, we constantly heard references to the 'Preble County Sasquatch' and discussions about where the creature was last seen. The scenario was very frustrating for our Investigations. Everywhere was signs of partygoers. We found fake footprints underneath the bridge with discarded beer cans. We even found a cardboard box hanging on an old fence saying: "Bigfoot Drinks Beer Here." Monitoring our radio did produce some local folklore, rumors and some substantiated reports of other strange occurrences.

A deputy (who asked to remain anonymous) told us of some past events that happened in the vicinity of the covered bridge.

"I haven't seen a deer in these parts lately. It just doesn't seem right, as they are usually plentiful in these parts.

We've also had reports of a wild goat or something roaming about. A couple of years ago, a young man hanged himself in a tree, he said."

Mr. L thought that maybe his son saw this wild goat up against a tree, but later dismissed that notion. The boy told me that he had seen this goat in the past and it was not the same thing he saw on the night in question.

Mrs. L told us that there were some rumors circulating the area about dead livestock. She was also aware of the local C.B.'ers claiming to have seen a hairy monster.

A month later, a cattle mutilation had taken place in West Alexandra, Ohio, just east of Eaton.

investigators talked with a local cattle breeder who was to produce Beefalo- a cross breed of cow and buffalo. The first birth of a calf was very exciting. Unfortunately, one morning, he found the calf dead in the barn. There was a hole in its chest and the heart had been removed. Whoever or whatever did this with surgical precision. The carcass showed the classic examples of the cattle mutilations that had been occurring in the western states.

Authorities hypothesized that there could be a devil cult in the area, but could not find any evidence. When the idea of a UFO connection crossed their mind, they contact the Ohio UFO Investigators League. The group didn't have any UFO reports from the area even though they canvassed the town and put ads in the local newspapers. Often times, strange lights have been reported, but this could be the result of nearby Wright-Patterson AFB. The case remains a mystery.

We found no evidence to suggest a connection to the purported sighting of a strange creature in Eaton. I only mention it here to show that this region has had some bizarre events.

Local History and Folklore

On old S.R. 725, just east of Camden is a summit along Paint Creek that is called the "Devil's Backbone." The steep gorge has several sharp turns, hence the name it receives. The area is engulfed with mystery and legends. There have been some strange, documented murders occurring during the 1800's.

Local legend has it that Miami Indian Chief Red Turtle cursed the area when driven west by the white men. According to the story:

The bones of Native American royalty reposed on Devil's Backbone and the white men were urged not to touch these bones. If they did, swift and merciless retribution would be forth coming. Ghost scouts are said to patrol the area."

Since many reports of this type occur near historical places, it is noteworthy to mention the Roberts Covered Bridge.

n 1829 after obtaining a contract from the U.S. government, Orlistus Roberts began building the bridge where the turnpike from Rossville crossed Seven Mile Creek on his property, in Section 14 of Gasper Township about 2.5 miles south of Eaton.

For nearly 160 years, Roberts Bridge remained in its original location. Many modifications and repairs were made, especially in 1962 and 1974.

On August 5, 1986, the bridge was vandalized that set on fire. Soon afterwards, a group of concerned citizens began restoration of the landmark. It was moved to Crystal Lake in Eaton in 1990. It is Ohio's oldest covered bridge and one of only six double- barreled bridges in the U.S.

Had we known that the figures were there the moment that I snapped the picture, we could have investigated further. Unfortunately, we did not have that opportunity, so many of these questions will remain forever unanswered.

Geographical Concerns

In geological terms, western Ohio is referred to as Glaciated Central Interior. The terra forming was the result of a glacier that came down towards the Ohio Valley. This end result caused much of this region to become flat with little rolling hills, much like the plains states.

The majority of Preble County is farming. During the summer, one can see corn and soybean fields for miles. There are small amounts of wooded terrain usually within the creeks, nature preserves and state parks, such as Hueston Woods.

There are many thriving businesses in the larger towns, such as Eaton - the county seat. As a matter of fact, there is a fertilizing plant just outside the city limits. Some major highways and railroads surround the county, as well as Dayton Ohio; just to the east in Montgomery County.

The region is not consistent with somewhere you would expect to produce Bigfoot reports, but there is access to other regions to the south with more foliage and less human population and development.

Conclusions and Opinion

This unusual report has many similarities to other so-called monster reports of the 70's. There is an abundance of reading material to educate interested parties with the subject. I have presented all the facts regarding the description and movements this entity reportedly did. The reader can except the testimony as valid or choose to ignore it.

I have often said, *"We investigate the reports of Bigfoot, not the creatures themselves."*

We can only speculate on the particulars until we have a specimen for scientific scrutiny. For the sake of this report and the many others of that time frame, it is imperative that we look into the sociological paradox that often encompasses the actual event.

Betty Parks and I compared notes on our separate interviews of the teens. Their stories seemed to coincide with just a few variations in their reporting. This is to be expected, as witness interpretation may vary with individuals. We felt the boys were telling the truth and believed they saw something strange and could not identify it, other than to say it was an ape.

Based upon our interviews, it became evident that the only preconceived notion was from the T.V. series, The Six Million Dollar Man." Other than that, they had no prior interest on the subject. There were no signs of any related paraphernalia in their homes. The Sheriff's Department believed the boy's testimony as well as other prominent citizens.

As far as we could ascertain, there was no publicity or rumors on the subject prior to the evening in question other than rumors about mutilated livestock. Local law enforcement had no records of devil cults within the county. The recent suicide of a man had no bearing on anything other than it just being strange because of the location.

The days after the report was made public, the community caught 'monster fever.' This was fueled by the newspaper accounts. It wasn't long before the account became the talk of the town and turned the local population into 'monster hunters.' The local C.B. channels sounded like military bands. It was almost to the point where one would think a local militia was being deployed.

This scenario would occur during the entire year in other sections of North America.

It was an investigative tragedy. With all the off-road vehicles, hikers and sightseers, if any hard evidence was there, it surely could have been destroyed. As I previously mentioned their signs were clearly visible. I found bogus footprints drawn into the creek bed sand, beer and soft drink cans and tire tracks all over the scene. Property owners told me of vandalism and damaged crops. Everybody was looking for Bigfoot. It did not matter if they believed the story or not. It was a great excuse to have something to do in their spare time. Suddenly, Bigfoot was in the subconscious of the community.

The only physical evidence we tagged were the two footprints found the following week. We could not locate any more prints or a trail. This could have been the result of the terrain, but it still has similarities to other reports of that year. I cannot even say with any accuracy that these prints were from the same individual that the two boys saw.

My dog did not act erratic when we found the tracks. As a matter of fact, D.B.'s dog was not excitable during the encounter. It just ran away from them before the sighting. T.L. told me that she always had a habit of running off. Historical accounts indicate that canines have an extreme fright of the creatures. In fact, none of the local domestic animals showed any unusual effects.

The greatest dilemma with this episode is the geographical location. This portion of Ohio is mainly farmland with some mild rolling hills. There are many tree lines and small wooded areas along the creeks. But, basically, the terrain is similar to the plains states.

This is not the type of environment one would expect to see an unknown hominid of the reported weight and height. As a general rule, the majority of reports originating in Ohio occur in the eastern portion of the state. That region is Appalachian foothills with an abundance of forested areas.

As far back as 1977, the region was surrounded by major highways, railroads and urban development. If a large creature, such as the one reported, wondered into Preble County, surely there would have been more reports come through. One could feasibly argue that some sightings went un-reported because of the ridicule factor. However, that is pure speculation. Therefore, this cannot be considered for evaluation of this report.

To familiarize the reader with the topography of land in question, please refer to figures 6.7.

The possibility of a hoax is something that can't be ignored. One has to remember that May is close to graduation for the Preble County high schools. Not far from the area, is Miami University located in Oxford. Pranks are always in abundance during this time of the year.

During my investigation, I checked the local costume shops and inquired about any ape disguises. I did not find any evidence of these types of rentals.

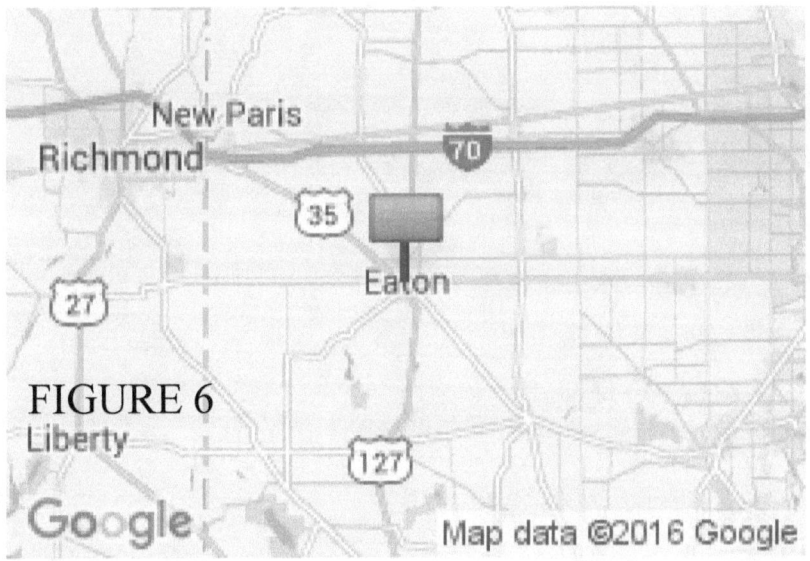

FIGURE 6

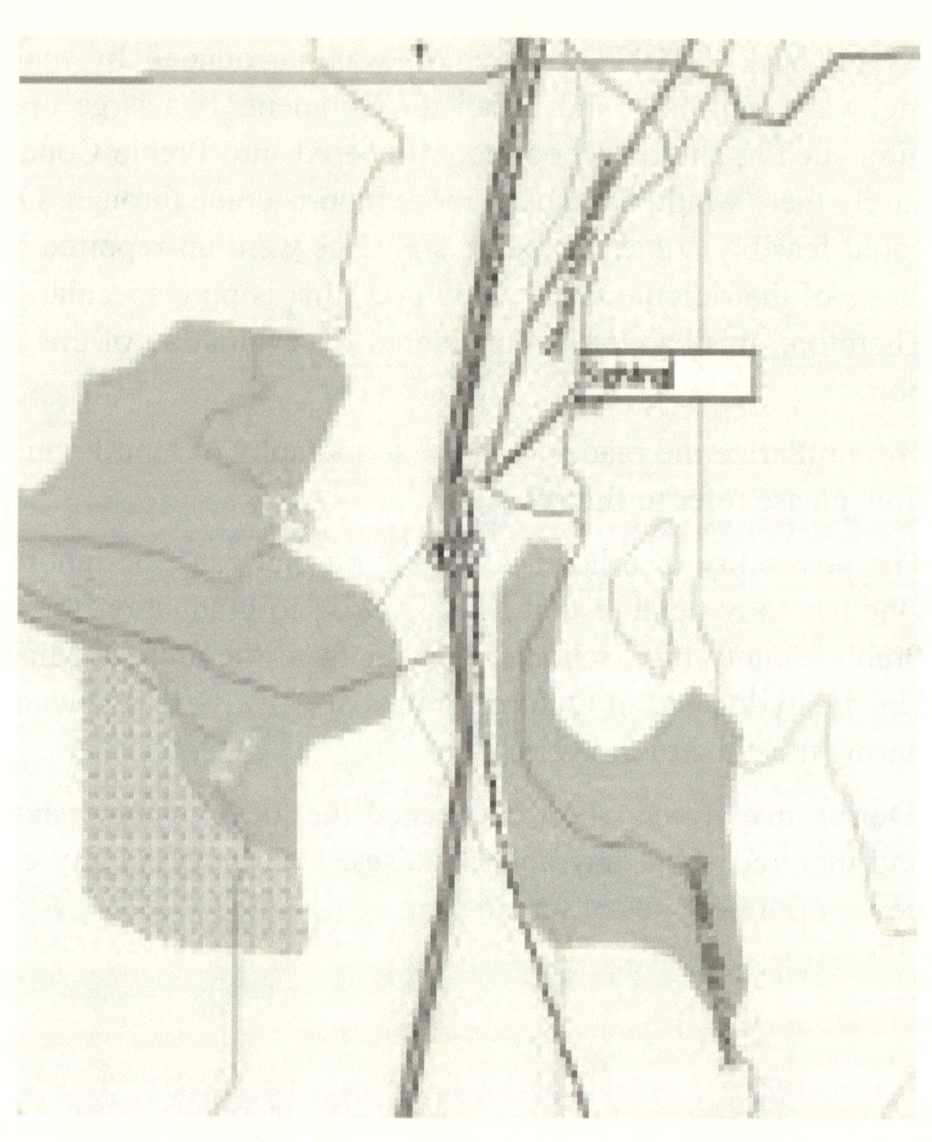

FIGURE 7

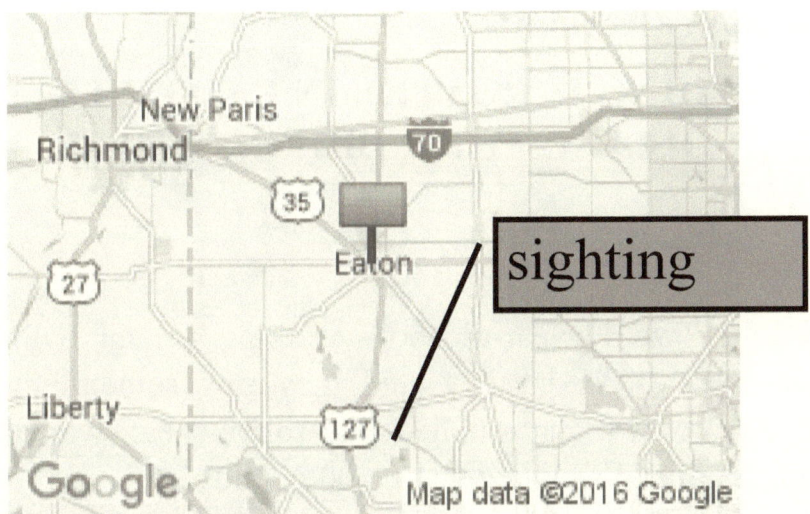

It should be mentioned that there are many landscaping firms in the area and a large fertilizer plant. During the heat and humidity of the summer, one can smell unpleasant orders, such as described by the witnesses and other residents.

It is my opinion that the boys did not perpetrate any kind of hoax. Their behavior and mannerisms to investigators, law enforcement, neighbors and parents lead me to conclude that they were being honest in what they reported. Therefore, one must conclude that they witnessed a bizarre event in which they perceived as a "bigfoot type" creature. The case remains unexplained. Since the trail went cold after the event, there is nothing more to establish at this point.

The sociological impact still haunts Preble County to this day. Follow up investigations by George Clappison in 1997 revealed that the local population still converse about reports of 'hairy monsters.' Many claim to have heard unusual sounds and something roaming about at night. That spring day in 1977 is still engulfed in the subconscious of the community.

Newspaper Accounts

SOMETHING IS ROTTEN IN EATON, TWO 13 -YEAR-OLDS REPORT; BIGFOOT' TALK START

EATON - Two 13-year-old boys walking through a Preble County woods Wednesday said they saw something that "had dirty brown fur, smelled like rotten meat, was about nine feet tall and weighed about 500 pounds."

Around the county, people have come to call the thing the Preble County Sasquatch, sheriff's dispatcher Greg Boerner said this morning.

Boerner said a small legend of a "Bigfoot" sighting is growing, although two deputies searched a thick woods about three miles south of downtown Eaton on Old Camden Pike and found nothing. The boys, whom deputies have not identified, report seeing the "thing" about 8:30 p.m. Wednesday.

Boerner said people in the county are unsure what to think about the report, but the boys are more decided. "They're scared to death," said Boerner.

"Whether they saw it or not, I don't know," he said. "Their mother called us and said they swore on a stack of Bibles that they saw it."

Source: Dayton, Ohio; Daily News; May 20, 1977

PREBLE AUTHORITIES GET REPORTS OF ' BIG FOOT'

EATON, Ohio - Preble County sheriff's deputies have received several reports of the county's own "Big Foot" apparently seen in the area of the Roberts Covered Bridge on Old Camden Pike, two miles south of here. Reports have been taken from persons who said they have seen a large, shaggy, foul-smelling creature. No one has obtained any photographs to substantiate the reports.

Source: Richmond, Indiana; Palladium-Item; May 25, 1977

NO "BIGFOOT," AUTHORITIES SAY

Two claimed sightings of the legend "Bigfoot" near the Roberts Covered Bridge have proven unfounded.

The first sighting came last Wednesday when two 13-year-old boys told sheriff's deputies they saw something that "had dirty brown fur, smelled like rotten meat, was about nine feet tall and weighed 500 pounds."

Deputies conducted a through search of the area and I "couldn't find a thing," according to Ron Hayes. He admitted, however, that the boys who reported the sightings "were really scared."

Another unconfirmed sighting was reported Saturday by some Eaton High School students. The Register-Herald has learned that some youths were putting masks on Sunday and Monday and walking the area, three miles south of Eaton near Old Camden Pike.

"Somebody could get hurt by doing that kind of thing," a sheriff's deputy said.

Deputies have stepped up patrolling in the area, not because of the sighting but because youths are trespassing and walking on newly planted crops.

Source: Eaton, Ohio; Register-Herald; May 25, 1977

References

Ron Schaffner

1.) The Robert's Covered Bridge was moved from its original location in 1990. It is now located in the southern portion of the Eaton city limits.

2.) Taped interviews with witness T.L and Betty Parks interviewing D.B. Recordings are on file.

3.) Email from Preble County historian Polly Kronenberger on 2/07/2001

4.)Preble County.com home page.

CHAPTER TEN
OHIO BIGFOOT IN THE NEWS

The Minnesota Weekly Record, January 23, 1869
(Direct quote from publication)

A GORILLA IN OHIO—Gallipolis (Ohio) is excited over a wild man, who is reported to haunt the woods near that city. He goes naked, is covered with hair, is gigantic in height, and "his eyes start from their sockets." A carriage, containing a man and daughter, was attacked by him a few days ago. He is said to have bounded at the father, catching him in a grip like that of a vice, hurling him to the earth, falling on him and endeavoring to bite and scratch like a wild animal. The struggle was long and fearful, rolling and wallowing in the deep mud, half suffocated, sometimes beneath his adversary, whose burning and maniac eyes glared into his own with murderous and savage intensity. Just as he was about to become exhausted from his exertions, his daughter, taking courage at the imminent danger of her parent, snatched up a rock and hurled it at the head of her father's would-be-murderer, was fortunate enough to put and end to the struggle by striking him, after which he slowly got up and retired into the neighboring copse that skirted the road

Comment: Stories of this nature are quite rare in association with Bigfoot. Usually Bigfoot creatures will not confront humans. They will either flee from humans to the safety of the forest, or they will take little notice of nearby humans and saunter nonchalantly away. This having been said, the article above is one example of the other Bigfoot extreme. Other examples throughout history have suggested that Bigfoot creatures have actually killed human beings.

The Akron, Ohio Beacon & Republican-Buckeye News, May 26, 1897

Farmers near Logan were greatly excited over the appearance of a strange animal in that vicinity. Numerous sheep and lambs had disappeared from many area farms. At night, farmers in the area could hear strange cries coming from the adjacent wooded area. Several old pioneers who had heard the cries of the beast at night said it was a panther, while others said the cries resembled that of a wild cat. Since numerous sheep had been missing, the farmers determined on a grand hunt for the beast in which every man who was able to carry a gun was to be pressed into service, with view of effecting the capture of the strange visitor.

The Cleveland Plain Dealer

Charles Lukins and Bob Forner, while cutting timber a few miles from Rome, claim they encountered a wild man. The men struggled with the wild man and after several attempts, they say that they were able to drive the gorilla-like creature into his supposed retreat among the cliffs. They described the terror as being about six feet tall and his only covering, apparently, a mat of long, curly hair.

The Cleveland Plain Dealer, June 16, 1897

Hopewell Township residents reported the appearance of a nude man in Ogle's woods. Reports claim that this man approached the public road twice in two days from these woods. He ran after an employee of Henry Creeger, who was driving, but fearing the nude man was demented, he drove away rapidly and the nude man was soon out of sight. The wife of Rev. G.A. Barlebaugh, accompanied by her little son, was returning to the city from the country when the man appeared wearing nothing but a hat. Mrs. Bartelbaugh became frightened and turned around and returned to the city over another road. Search parties attempted to capture the man to discover whether he is wild or insane, but as of yet, they have not been able to apprehend the man.

Comment: From the description given in this account, it appears fairly obvious that we have a case involving a "wild man." However, it is interesting to note that on the west coast, Indians have referred to Sasquatch as "the big man with the little hat." This description results from the creature's sagital crest (pointed head) which from a distance appears to resemble a little hat. Since Mrs. Bartelbaugh described the man as wearing a hat, it becomes apparent that although this is probably a story about a deranged human who ran about the town without clothes on, it may have a correlation with Bigfoot.

The New York Globe

Three citizens in Union County claim they each watched an enormous, strange-looking creature emerge from different wooded areas. The first witness, Patrick Poling, said the monster was "about seven feet tall and could weigh 400 pounds." Poling was plowing a field one evening before dusk when the beast burst out of the woods and lumbered along the edge of the clearing. He watched the creature until it was about 100 feet from him. The creature then turned and looked at him and then ran into the woods. Poling states that the creature looked like a big hairy ape that walked like a man. He said it had long black hair that was unlike fur since it hung straight down. Poling then rushed to a neighbor's house to report the amazing scene. The next day, Poling and a few neighbors went in search of the beast. Near the edge of the woods, they found three huge four-toed footprints. A plaster cast was made of the prints. It measures 17 inches long, 7 inches wide, and two inches deep.

Experts from the Mammal Research Team in Lima, Ohio, who specialize in tracking wild creatures that kill farm animals, rushed to Union County in hopes of spotting the beast. Team leader, Bill Sheets, stated he had between 150 and 200 documented sightings of a similar creature in other areas of Ohio and has himself spotted the hairy beast three times. He stated that the Union County sighting fits the overall description of a giant, ape-like creature that has been seen many times before throughout the state.

Less than a week later, residents of nearby Logan County claimed they saw a hulking shape rush into the woods late one night. Two days after this, Donna Riegler of Marysville, Ohio, said she was returning home from work when she saw a gigantic, hairy creature lying on the highway. She was so frightened she put her car into reverse and backed away from the beast. Riegler reported that it was covered with hair and it stumbled away with a robot-like walk. The Union County Sheriff's Department put several officers on the case and stated there was no doubt in their minds that somebody saw something "out there." Officials at the Columbus Zoo in Ohio were given a cast of a footprint for study.

Cincinnati Post and Times Star, January 30 to February 3, 1959

A trucker reported to police that he saw a hulking creature climb out of the Ohio River onto the shore at Cincinnati. It was a cold night and a violent wind was whipping the river into six-foot waves. The trucker refused to describe the monster to police, but more calls came in. Across the river at Covington, Kentucky, a motorist reported seeing a thing on two legs, three or four times the size of a man and much bulkier, on a bridge over the Licking River.

Strange Creatures from Time and Space Magazine, March 28, 1959

A seven-foot "thing" covered with grey hair and having large luminous eyes was reported near Mansfield, Ohio. *Comment: Another report of a similar creature in this area was received in 1963.*

Cleveland Plain Dealer, August, 1972

A seven-foot creature covered in black hair was seen in the woods behind the Cleveland Zoo. A resident, Wayne E. Lewis, said he encountered the creature at 9:30 p.m., while looking for a kitten. It was standing behind a fence and was a lot bigger than he was. Mr. Lewis, a sixfoot tall man himself, gave his own weight at 360 pounds. A 19-year old youth, who also saw the creature, said it looked like a gorilla except that it stood straighter.

Cleveland Plain Dealer, November 30, 1972

A cab driver reported to police at Ironton, Ohio, that he saw a large white ape-like thing dragging a dog or deer. Ironton is on the Ohio River at the south edge of Wayne National Forest in Lawrence County. Comment: *There have been several other Bigfoot reports of note in that immediate area. One occurred on 2/24/1991 in Wayne National Forest just northwest of Ironton. Another occurred in August of 1980 off of State Route 93 just north of Ironton. Another sighting occurred even more recently just across the river from Ironton, just south of Ashland Kentucky. This sighting occurred in August of 1998.*

Sighting Investigation by Albert Hartman, August, 1973

Just north of Mansfield, a man saw an eight-foot creature, very wide and with very long arms, standing by his barn at about 2:00 a.m. After watching it for several moments, he shot at it with a shotgun in order to frighten the creature away. It worked, and the creature fled the man's property. He reported the incident to the local sheriff.

Akron Beacon Journal, August 27, 1973

Several residents of Massillon, Ohio reported seeing a seven-foot hairy monster. They reported that the monster exuded a very strong odor. The police were notified of this sighting and investigated accordingly.

The Michigan Anomaly Research, October 15, 1973

A series of witnesses, including two security guards, reported seeing an eight-foot hairy monster around a golf course in the Dublin vicinity. A spokesperson for the Franklin County Sheriff's Department said that guards had spotted this monster on at least three different occasions— once standing in the roadway, next in a cemetery near the golf course, and the last time running away. A sheriff's lieutenant and sergeant spent several hours investigating the incident and questioning the security guards, who were reportedly very frightened. The guards were employees of Able Detective & Security Systems. They were assigned to guard the Jack Nicklaus Golf Course, which was under construction northwest of Dublin. The guards carried rifles since a farmer reported seeing the monster near a fairway on the golf course. The guards told deputies that they looked up and saw the thing standing by a big tree. It fled silently when it saw them. A footprint found along the creek bank resembled a human foot except that it appeared to have three toes or claws. The entire footprint was about a foot long and seven inches wide. The security firm supervisor said that since they first sighted the monster, he has doubled up the guards on duty at the golf course and armed them with rifles.

Cleveland Magazine, October, 1973

At about 2:00 on an August morning, at Oberlin, a man named Rudy Randolph and five other raccoon hunters saw an eight-foot, shaggy haired, stinking animal with red glowing eyes. The hunter's dogs crowded the creature into a cornfield, but as the men returned to their cars, the creature turned back and began chasing them. Police investigated and found footprints in the vicinity but they were not clear enough to cast; however, it was determined from the footprints that the creature was bipedal and had a five-foot stride.

Sighting Investigation by Tom Archer, September, 1974

Footprints, 14 inches long and six inches wide showing five toes were seen and photographed in a field close to some woods near Westerville, Ohio in Delaware County just north of Columbus.

Sighting Investigation by Don Worley, July 10, 1975

Two ten-year-old children were playing on a farm in Preble County. They saw a strange creature watching them over the top of six-foot corn stalks. They ran and got a 12-year-old friend who also saw the creature. They tried to get the father of the older child to come and investigate, but he paid no attention to them. The children then climbed up on a shed roof and watched the creature. After a while, the creature ran off towards some woods and disappeared. The children described the creature as being upright, leaning slightly forward, and covered in long, smooth brown hair.

Journal Herald, February 7, 1977

Tracks measuring 20 inches by 6 inches of an unknown creature were found in snow beside a mobile home. The tracks led investigators up a hill and they seemed to proceed with very large strides. Investigators followed the tracks for almost a mile before the tracks disappeared completely into bushy woods.

Record Courier, March 10, 1977

Mrs. Barbara Pistilli of Nelson Township, Portage County, telephoned the sheriff's office on March 8, 1977 and stated that two teenagers had seen and shot at a giant furry creature. Deputies were told that the creature was eight feet tall with an estimated weight of 500 pounds. The creature walked out of the woods and started across a field. It fled when shots were fired at it. Mrs. Pistilli stated that other people in the area had seen the creature before.

Homestead City News, August 29, 1977

Dean Averick, a Florida resident, stated that he had seen a Sasquatch when he operated Deans' Boat Landing near Padanaram, Ohio in 1954. He said he saw a hairy creature that had a snub nose, peaked eyes, was very chesty, had light-brown scraggly hair, was over six feet tall, and had a long straight back. It walked out of the brush about 125 yards up the shoreline and waded into about three feet of water, then, "I figured it must have seen me," Averick said, "because it headed for a small island off shore.

The Columbus Dispatch, July 16, 1978 (Para-Hominoid Research, Dispatch State Service)

Residents of Butler reported seeing a mysterious creature. Acting police chief Phil Stortz investigated the incident and stated that the creature did leave an impression in the grass. The imprint was very large, and some unusual hair was found on a bush nearby. According to Stortz, a dog owned by a local resident jumped through the picture window of his owner's home after seeing something and ran around erratically inside the house. No one is sure exactly what the dog saw, but the dog was obviously very frightened.

Stortz went on to say that it has been hard to come up with a good description of the creature because the sightings have all occurred at night. He noted that the creature might be a deer or some other regular inhabitant of the hilly woods throughout the area around Mohican State Park near the Butler community of 1,300. So far, he said there have been "three or four confirmed sightings" in the area. The Richland County Sheriff's Department said at least three reports of sightings were made in the vicinity of the Roger Kline home. Several members of the Kline family have seen the creature. Stortz has also heard of a half-dozen sightings that were not reported to the police.

Mount Vernon News, July 18, 1978

A Knox County sheriff deputy investigated a traffic accident on Ohio 95 near the Richland County line. Upon arriving on the scene, the deputy said he found a badly frightened young man who was "so scared that he scared me." The man told the deputy he ran off the pavement because he saw Bigfoot on the roadway. "It was as big as a bear on its hind legs," the man told the deputy. The skeptical deputy began his routine accident investigation despite the incredulous protests of the man who could not believe the deputy was refusing to check the adjacent woods. Since that incident, three sightings occurred in Richland County of a "creature" seven to nine feet tall, with red eyes and a head as large as a tractor tire. The latest sighting was by a young girl who was badly shaken afterwards.

The Knox deputy who handled the Ohio 95 accident stated he is not so sure that the man in the accident was lying because he saw the creature before the sightings in Richland County. There was a report that a loose bear was captured in Ashland County but the story could not be confirmed. If a bear was in the southern-most area of Ashland County, it could be responsible for the sightings. But then again, it may not have been a bear at all but some other unknown creature.

The Cleveland Plain Dealer, August 24, 1978

Six residents of Paris Township reported they saw a 6-foot tall creature covered with hair sitting atop a backyard chicken co-op at the home of a Mr. and Mrs. Herbert Cayton. One of the witnesses drove a car across the backyard with its headlights on to get a better look at the creature. When the creature ran towards the car, the five other witnesses ran into the Cayton house. The creature then began looking in the window at them. Facial features could not be seen because of the creature's bushy hair. The group also heard footsteps on the roof, but when Mrs. Cayton loaded a gun, the creature disappeared into the woods. The sheriff was called to investigate, and he stated that when he arrived, the people were visibly shaken and some were even afraid to go to sleep. There were two footprints found—one distinguishable, the other not so good. The sheriff scouted the heavily wooded area but found no sign of the creature. Mr. and Mrs. Cayton said they had seen the creature several times over the past few months. Four other residents said they had seen the creature and two similar but smaller creatures on a previous occasion.

The Ligonier Echo, May 24, 1995-Samuel Sherry Sr.

There is a place known as The Bigfoot Camp in Dry Run and Shirey's Run near the Black Swamp. The Black Swamp consists mostly of wetlands and has a large population of skunk cabbage. The large amount of Bigfoot evidence that has been collected here is often attributed to the Bigfoot's propensity to eat the skunk cabbage. Footprints that were eighteen inches long with five distinct toes were discovered in the area. Also, a photo which could possibly be of Bigfoot in heavy foliage was taken in the area. People will also often times report hearing strange screams coming from the forest at night. There is also an adequate water source at the remains of an old reservoir which exists in the area. The area is closed to the general public as well as motor traffic. These are generally considered disruptive to the habitat of the creature. Only people hunting for Bigfoot are allowed to roam the area. Large primate handprints were also found in mud near a tree in Liverpool, Ohio.

THE SEMI-WEEKLY AGE.

COSHOCTON, OHIO, FRIDAY, JANUARY 28, 1887.

Spring Mountain.

Our trappers are having considerable bother with an unknown animal that gobbles up the traps, but in every instance leaves the bait untouched. It seems to be a very cunning animal too, because it lately left three traps hidden very nicely under some old clapboards.

NEWARK DAILY ADVOCATE.

NEWARK, OHIO. FRIDAY, AUGUST 3. 1888.

THOSE TRACKS.

Strange Phenomena Showing a Giant's Foot Prints.

Curious Sight in Front of Carrol's Store.—A Race of Extinct Giants.

One of the curious things to be seen about Newark is on the side walk fronting the Columbus store. If you have never noticed it, stop as you go along and look down. There you will see the foot prints of a giant, who, perchance made tracks in the Devonian age. It is not impossible that this enormous foot print, which shows that it must have been made by a man at least ten feet high, may prove a key to unlock some more of nature's laboratory for geologists. Here is a silent revelation of geological epochs, a mysterious link to join the past with the present. Whether that foot print was planted there before the Noachian deluge, or that stone was once an avenue in ancient Pompeii, no one can tell. Sacred writ records the flood though traditions from Ovid's myth of Deucalion and Pyrrah, and from nations as cultured as the Greeks and Romans down to barbar tribes and those of the fierce Koloschian of Alaska, yet there are doubts of the Mosaic flood being universal, and the giant who stamped his foot upon that strata of rock may have escaped the overwhelming tide. For every layer of rock there are cemeteries of generations of little creatures which well enjoyed life and its freedom. This may be nature's method of issuing her bulletins along her march of time to disclose to man her mysterious work. Neither the catacombs, with their mute representations "of grinning skulls with teeth all natural but preserving their smile," nor the Egyptian Pyramids, and other wonderous works of man are more impressive than that foot print which show in chronological order the wear and tear of the Cycles of Time. Doubtless the race of giants of which this is a representative would make Goliath of Gath look like a Lilliputian and greatly belittle the job David done, and for which he is now getting so much credit. These stange tracks and foot prints are certainly as mysterious as the Old Fort.

The Salem Daily News.

SALEM, OHIO, THURSDAY, AUGUST 27, 1891.

Is It Wild Man or Beast?

MARTINS FERRY, O., Aug. 27.—The farmers near Negee, this county, have organized to hunt down the wild man or animal that has been killing and devouring sheep, hogs, chickens. etc., in that section. Many of the farmers are afraid to work in their fields, go out after their stock or go to sleep at night, fearing they will be killed. The wild man or whatever it is has been seen by Samuel Crow and others. Crow says it is covered with dark reddish hair, has large ears, small eyes, teeth like those of a wild boar, huge mouth and paws, measures about five feet in height and weighs fully 200 pounds. It is said that the animal walks and runs as well on two as four legs, can climb a tree or hill quickly and is seen only in the morning and evening. Farmers and their families in the vicinity are very much frightened.

THE SALEM DAILY NEWS.

SALEM, OHIO, TUESDAY EVENING, FEBRUARY 2, 1897.

WILD MAN.

People of Danville Terrorized—Schools Closed—Small Child Seized.

Coshocton, February 2.—Word has reached here of the queer doings of a wild man who has been terrorizing the village of Danville and vicinity. He is described as being of more than ordinary hight, with a long flowing mane springing from between his shoulders. He is clad only from his hips down with the pelts of sheep.

George Welker, a farmer, first saw him and gave pursuit, but was distanced. The man was tracked to a hut and when a posse went to it he was absent. When he returned those who had been keeping watch reported it and the wild man was pursued by men on horseback, but he escaped. The cabin was fitted up with sheep pelts. Once when chased he eluded his pursuers, although carrying a sheep under his arm. The schools in the terrorized territory were closed, as the people were afraid to send their children after the man seized a child going to school and ran with it a half mile before releasing it.

THE MARION DAILY STAR.

MARION, OHIO, THURSDAY, JUNE 10, 1897.

WILD MAN SEEN AGAIN.

He Wears Nothing but Hair, Which Is Long and Curly.

The wild man who created so much terror among the inhabitants near Rome, O., several weeks ago by his strange actions has again been seen. Charles Lukins and Bob Forner, while cutting timber a few miles from Rome, claim they encountered a wild man and after a severe struggle say they were able to drive the gorillalike object into his supposed retreat among the cliffs.

They describe the terror as being about six feet tall and his only covering, apparently, a mat of long, curly hair. From their description of the supposed wild man he is undoubtedly the same seen a number of times several weeks ago.

Women and children are now more thoroughly frightened than ever and are afraid to venture from their homes lest they meet the wild creature. A posse of determined men will scour the country now until the terror is located and captured or killed. — Cleveland Plain Dealer.

The Massillon Independent.

MASSILLON, OHIO, THURSDAY AUGUST 10, 1899.

REIGN OF TERROR.

Stories of the Wild Man of the Woods.

WHAT THE POSSE FOUND.

Hacked Trees and Holes in the Ground Left Behind by One Who, in his Fighting Fits Attacks the Nearest Objects.

The reign of terror of the wild man of the rail timber north west of Jersey remains unbroken. Every day parties of Massillon, West Brook and Sippo citizens scour the woods, thrusting long poles into all suspicious places too dark to be explored by the eye but without succeeding in so much as catching sign of their quarry. Constable Sibea(?) of West Brookfield, who led one posse through the timberland is in Massillon today. He says they found trees which had be hacked with a hatchet and holes in the ground too large to be those of animals, but the wild man himself evaded them entirely. It is the popular supposition that this violent individual carries a long handled hatchet which he wields with intense fury, attacking trees and the earth when other foes are lacking.

A telephone message that this man of the woods had been located near the rolling mill caused Policeman Ertle(?) to hurry thither the other day. When he arrived, an individual sitting under a tree in a nearby grove was pointed out to him. "He's crazy, officer he's crazy, he' crazy." the workmen declared. Which remark caused the policeman to lay a hand on his shooting irons and then with firm tread proceed to the grove. The man under the tree looked up over the copy of the "Christian Advocate" he was reading, and greeted the officer pleasantly. He said he was a stranger in the city and was in hard luck. He and the officer came down town together and from here the stranger went to Canton where he was hopeful of securing employment. The policeman was disgusted with the whole affair and he now takes the wild man stories with a grain of salt.

The Massillon Independent.

MASSILLON, OHIO, MONDAY AUGUST 14, 1899.

SEVERAL SAW HIM.

Terror of the Woods Takes to the City.

WAS SEEN IN MILL STREET.

Mrs. Nicholas Krell and Her Son Declare He Visited Their Home Thursday Night—Marshal Kitchen Makes an Investigation.

Mrs. Nicholas Krell, of 353 North Mill street, is a sister of Miss Matilda Ries of Crystal Spring, who is in a critical condition from injuries sustained at the hands of a human brute while walking home from Massillon a few days ago. Thursday evening Mrs. Krell was at home with her four small children, her husband being employed at night at one of the near-by coal mines. At 8 o' clock Mrs. Krell, who was removing some screens in the north part of the house, heard her 4-year-old son, Leo, scream. She hurried to him, and he declared that he had seen the wild man. "He came right up to the screen door and was going to come in when I cried." said the child.

Mrs. Krell took the boy in her arms and went to the front part of the house. Glancing around the corner, she too, saw the wild man. "He was under the grape arbor and was running fast,' declares Mrs. Krell 'He seemed to be dressed, and he seemed tall, but further I can't describe him. I don't think much about this wild man business, but I do think it is someone who has a grudge against our family."

Marshal Kitchen arrive at 9 o'clock, and he looked all over the neighborhood, but without finding a trace of the intruder. Mrs. Krell refused to remain in her home over night. With her children she went to the residence of Mrs. Wittmann, a neighbor. When she returned this morning she found the front door of her home standing wide open. She is doubtful whether she closed it the night before, but the children declare she did. Nothing was missing. About a year ago burglars entered the Krell residence, while Mrs. Krell and the child were there, and stole much.

Mrs. Arnold Scllberger, of 314 North Mill street, declares she saw the wild man Thursday afternoon. She was picking berries in a cornfield in the rear of the Krell property when she came across him. Just what he looked like, she can not say, for her eye had no sooner fallen upon him than she ran home as fast as she could.

THE LIMA TIMES-DEMOCRAT.

LIMA, OHIO, THURSDAY, AUGUST 1, 1901.

"WILD MAN"

Was the Invention of Crowd of Berry Pickers.

They Found a Patch of Blackberries and Wanted to Keep Others Away from the Placc.

Special by wire to Times-Democrat.

Bereau, O., Aug. 1.—Newspapers of the state have been full of stories about a "wildman" terrorizing the community. It was a scheme of berry pickers who had found a nice patch of black berries and rigged up a wild man to keep others away. Since a posse has been on the trail of the alleged wild man, he has kept under cover.

THE LIMA TIMES-DEMOCRAT.

LIMA, OHIO, MONDAY, APRIL 14, 1902.

THE PUMA OUTDONE.

Rockport and Beaverdam People Have a New Freak to be Afraid of.

Not since the time, several years ago, when Charley Price's famous mythical puma had the natives of the Putnam county swamps dodging their own shadows has a scare been started in northwestern Ohio to equal that now in full sway in the vicinity of the village of Rockport and Beaver Dam. The puma will have to take a back seat for the new freak, an account of which appeared in the following dispatch from Columbus Grove to the Enquirer:

"A strange being, apparently half man, and half beast, is seen in the county round about Rockport and Beaver Dam. The creature puts in an appearance at or near farmhouses.

"For some time the farmers in that vicinity have been troubled by nightly visits, apparently from intruders bent on securing money or other valuables. It was the scheme of the prowler to attempt to open a window or fumble at the door locks, then move on to the rear part of the house, and after giving the gates and such outposts a good shake disappears as quickly as he came. The family of Frank Conkleman left their home because of these visits, and while they were gone the strange being was seen.

"The creature is described as resembling a man, although possesses of features coarse and rough, and is said to be covered with hair. The inhabitants of that staid old country vicinity are half crazed with excitement, and the female portion will not venture outside after nightfall.

"It is firmly believed that the strange creature is an insane person who has been at large for some time. The being is attired in dress peculiar to one of the male sex, although scantily clad. A searching party will be organized to capture the fellow, if possible, although his fleetness of foot and abilities at fence jumping almost preclude any idea of so doing."

THE NEWARK ADVOCATE

NEWARK, OHIO, WEDNESDAY EVENING, OCTOBER 12, 1904.

WILD MAN

SCARING PEOPLE IN VICINITY OF NEW PHILADELPHIA.

As Big as Goliath, Fleet as the Wind and Lithe as the Deer is at Large.

New Philadelphia, O., Oct. 12–The people of this community are greatly exercised over the stories related by wayfarers that a wild man, who haunts are the woods, is at large. Mothers have warned their boys and girls to keep within calling distance. While their fathers are on the lookout for the creature that has suddenly become a menace to hickory nut parties.

The wild man is said to be a giant in stature and to roam about without a stitch of clothing on his body. As fleet as the wind and lithe as the deer he has so far outdistanced the swiftest hounds that have been put on his trail by their masters. Some men all but cornered him Monday night, but were afraid to tackle him. He tore up a handful of grass and munched it while the hunters where in view. Then he ran away.

THE LIMA NEWS

LIMA, OHIO, SATURDAY, JANUARY 10, 1914.

VIGILANTES TRY FOR "WILD MAN"

WOMEN ABROAD AT NIGHT ARE FRIGHTENED BY QUEER PERSON

New York, Jan. 9.—Alarmed by the repeated reports that a "wild man" is terrorizing lone women by night the young men of the Church of the Hold Child Jesus at Richmond Hill, L. I., have organized a vigilance band to seize the mysterious person.

According to the stories of the women he is said to have accosted, her invariably wears a long tan overcoat. Under it is something that looks like a woman's garment. Some say the marauder has a beard. Others say he is clean shaven. At the approach of a man he takes to his heels. He is reported to have been seen in several parts of the town on the same night.

The women of Richmond Hill are so nervous that the local police say they think some of the reported appearances are hallucinations. Mrs. Martin J. Sgier, wife of Dr. Sgier, says, however, that she is positive the fellow frightened her and if the Vigilance Committee catches him she will appear in court as a complainant.

The "wild man" has made a specialty of harassing the woman members of the congregation of the Church of the Holy Child Jesus, of which Father Nummey is rector. The attendance at early mass, held before daybreak when the phantom is most active, fell off so that Father Nummey complained to the Mayor that the police were not doing their duty. Detective Hoffman was assigned to stop the annoyance, but did not succeed.

THE SANDUSKY STAR-JOURNAL

THURSDAY, SEPT. 28, 1916

Frank Johnson, farmer, residing north of Fremont, reports a strange monkey is running at large in the neighborhood where he lives. It is thought that the monk escaped from one of the shows at the Sandusky-co fair last week, says a Fremont paper.

REV. HOOD SAYS APE HE SAW WAS ONLY AN ORDINARY GROUNDHOG

Minister Expresses Surprise That Innocent People Should be Terrified by Wild Story for which he Declares There is no Foundation in Fact.

Declaring that the statement that he saw an ape near Walhonding or anywhere else, and that the whole story was manufactured out of the whole cloth, Rev. C. H. Hood, of Coshocton, expressed his regret that anything so preposterous should be foisted upon the people of the county. Friday, Mr. Hood returned late Thursday from Bryesville where he attended the funeral of his brother. He had been gone since Monday.

"It is unfair to the people of the Walhonding community to circulate such a story," said Mr. Hood. "People up there are afraid to let their children get out of their sight for fear this mysterious animal will capture them. The whole community is terrified, and for my part I do not want to be included in any such group of alarmists. What I saw was a large groundhog, and I called it that at the time. At no time have I even intimated that it was anything else, and obviously I have taken no part in conferences with the county officials, having been out of town since Monday.

"I wish you would correct the impression that I was a party to the circulation of this wild rumor," he told a reporter. He also stated emphatically that he could not account for the report given the paper.

The report that an ape had escaped from a Cleveland zoo and had been sighted in at least two central Ohio communities, the last of which was near Walhonding, had its effect. A camping party west of Walhonding and near the spot where the animal was reported to have been seen, broke camp Friday morning. People in the neighborhood were sticking close to their homes or going armed. Blackberry picking had ceased for miles around, while the sole topic of conversation was the ape.

Wild stories of a man having been killed near Dennison by the animal, the serious injury of a woman berry picker in Tuscarawas-co. and the capture of the ape near Cavallo sprang up like mushrooms Friday and spread like wildfire. It is doubtful if anything has so stirred the county in months. In many communities and throuot Coshocton groups of men and boys were feverishly discussing means of capturing the animal and claiming the $2000 reward, alleged to have been offered for its return to Cleveland alive.

R. B. Gauley and John Branfield, who told the story in Coshocton, stuck to their original statements Friday.

Rev. Hood, who is a partner of Mr. Gauley's in the insurance business said Friday that he was hunting groundhogs when he spied the animal and attempted to stalk it. He said he carried a rifle of .22 caliber, and was too far away to risk a shot. When he started to creep up on his game he declares Mr. Gauley insisted it was not a groundhog. Hood declared he laughed to himself and went on, but was unable to get within gunshot of the animal before it disappeared into the bushes.

"I did throw a stone into the underbrush in an effort to start the groundhog, but there was no 'monkey chattering' reply." Hood asserted. "I naturally dismissed the matter from my mind and thot no more about it until upon arriving home late Thursday to be confronted with this harrowing tale. People kept my telephone ringing last night until after 11 o'clock, wanting to know all about the 'ape.' I have been forced to leave the house to avoid the continual nuisance," he declares.

Coshocton Tribune

TUSCARAWAS-CO APE WAS A DEACON ARRAYED IN BUFFALO ROBE AND RED STAGE WHISKERS

That the ferocious man eating ape at large in the wilds of Tuscarawasco was only a humankind dressed up in a fur robe and whiskers for the purpose of keeping folks out of his berry patch is the purport of a tale coming out of New Philadelphia, which appeared in a Columbus paper of recent date. The story follows:

A man eating ape of ferocious mien is at large in the Beaver Dam valley and the countryside goes armed. Barn dances and box socials have been abandoned, the old swimming hole is deserted and the strategy board that was wont to meet nightly in Si Kummer's general store has adjourned sine die.

After nightfall there is not a soul stirring in the cities and even the dogs and cats, sensing the unknown terror, no longer roam the hills or scamper atop the fences.

With human cunning the ape has succeeded in keeping himself hidden from humankind. Of all the several scores who have sensed his presence, not one will admit having seen the fugitive. They know he is in the vicinity and do not care to investigate any further. The only authentic information that reaches the valley is that a huge ape owned by a carnival company, escaped from Cleveland several weeks ago.

WANT APE ARRESTED

Yesterday two women living in the neighborhood drove in town and demanded warrants for the arrest of the ape from County Prosecutor E. F. Lindsey. The prosecutor interviewed the sheriff, who informed him that his deputies were planning to go on a vacation and that the sheriff's rheumatism precluded him from taking the assignment personally.

So the warrants were refused and the women returned to the valley vowing they would not send their children to school or come to town to trade until the menace is removed.

Last Thursday Mrs. Ezra Butts had an encounter with a strange apparition near Conesville. Mrs. Butts was picking blackberries along the roadside and was attracted by a particularly tempting growth of briars in the Smuckfinckle woods. The woods have long been posted against trespassing, but Mrs. Butts places not trust in signs as between neighbors. She was rapidly filling her gallon pail, when a wild looking figure arose from behind a stump and growled several times.

At the first growl Mrs. Butts took the fence like a steeple chaser and before the second could be uttered she was well on her way home. When she and her breath had once again caught up with each other, she related her experience to her family, and they, her oldest son, who had been told at Pete Ward's blacksmith shop, that there was a reward of $2000 for the capture of the ape, dead or alive, sallied forth with a shotgun.

SAW STRANGE SIGHT

Ike scoured the Smuckfinckle woods and gradually worked his way to the berry patch. Dozing atop the trunk of a fallen tree the huntsman saw a strange hairy being, that did and did not resemble a man. From an elongated jaw, which seemed to be in spasmodic motion, were suspended a bristling set of red whiskers. Tufts of green hair shrouded the eyes, which burned with a purplish pale, eve in slumber. Over the entire body was a mat of reddish brown hair, save for the lower legs and foot which strange to behold were encased in a pair of rubber boots.

Ike decried that apes were not game, and must not therefore be shot on the wing, so he let drive with both barrels of his 12 gauge gun. His nerves shaken by the unholy mystery his first shot missed, but his second did not.

With a wild lashing and thrashing the strange being, freed from the tree stump and shrieking, disappeared into the briars. Ike followed after a precautionary trauma and in a clearing abruptly came upon Deacon Smuckfinckle picking a hatful of buckshot out of his rubber boots and adjacent territory. At his side lay the buffalo robe and a set of stage whiskers.

Being a typical Beaver Valley neighbor, Ike assisted the deacon in re-establishing an area of comfort, helped him home and went on his way reconstructing his plans to encompass a deficit of $2000 in his dream capitol.

The deacon explains from his nest of sofa cushions that he wanted to scare "them drafted boys out of the berry patch" and hadn't counted on Mrs. Butts or Ikey uor the escaped man eating ape.

The Lima News

AND TIMES-DEMOCRAT

LIMA, OHIO, THURSDAY, JULY 15, 1920

BIG APE ROAMS NEAR MARIETTA

Animal Escaped From Zoo or Circus is Hunted

MARIETTA, Ohio.–If the Cincinnati Zoo or any rambling circus that has passed thru Ohio have lost a first class Man-sized ape, disturbed residents of this town and the vicinity of Gravel Bank would like to have representatives come here and inquire into the antecedents of a strange animal that has stirred the quiet folk hereabouts to a high pitch of excitement.

Rumors of what is declared to be a large specimen of the African ape, seen in a heavy woods near Gravel Bank, eight mile below here on the Ohio river, have been confirmed by the weird experience of many people. The animal is declared to have on a number of occasions disputed the right of road with persons walking in the direction of Marietta.

The other night the strange animal is declared by Archie Cassady of Marietta to have squatted in the road and to have refused to permit Cassady and his party to pass. When the party offered to give the animal the road, the ape calmly moved over in front of them and blocked their passage. They returned later with an armed searching party, but the beast had disappeared. Another posse was organized after the people on a train, returning home, had seen the ape. but tho they found huge tracks in the under brush, the animal evidently had taken to the trees.

Several persons have fired at the animal, including William Fish, a farmer living near Gravel Bank. When frightened, those who have seen the animal report that the ape swings into the trees, jumping from branch to branch.

The ape is said to be considerably larger than a man, apparently being seven feet tall. It has not attacked any persons or livestock, and it is believed it hunts human habitation more from a desire for companionship than with the purpose of harm. When last seen the ape appeared to be well fed and at home in the woods he has selected as his habitat..

THE CHRONICLE-TELEGRAM

ELYRIA, OHIO, FRIDAY, JUNE 6, 1930

Ape Terrifies Norwalk

NORWALK, O., June 6.—Terrified residents of Norwalk today were barring doors and windows and afraid to leave their homes on the report that a large ape was seen running wild near the Memorial hospital.

Police and deputies began a systematic search for the beast after it was authentically reported that a dog was seen fighting with the animal.

The hospital area is near the Norwalk city limits. It is believed tho ape escaped from a circus which showed here about 10 days ago.

The animal was seen last in the garden of John Loudoll, just over the corporation line. Many other persons reported seeing the beast in a woods nearby.

A party of Detroit motorists parked along the road yesterday was frightened when the animal appeared near the highway and notified the sheriff's office. A search failed to find any trace of the ape.

Attaches of the hospital also have told police of seeing the animal near the building.

The Coshocton Tribune

SATURDAY EVENING, JUNE 7, 1930.

Army of Ape-Hunters Search North Ohio for Anthropoid

NORWALK. O., June 7. — An army of ape-hunters, a new kind of searching party in Ohio, is combing northern Ohio today for a large anthropoid ape, which is reported to be roaming this secion.

Residents in the vicinity of Norwalk are horror-stricken following the many persistent reports of the huge animal's roaming activities.

First reports came from a party of motorists from Detroit. They said they had seen the ape. Monday, near the Norwalk Memorial hospital. Local residents scoffed at the news. Impossible, was the common opinion.

A tourist from Mansfield gave the next report. He said he saw the beast in the outskirts of the city. Many truck drivers and motorists made similar reports. Norwalk citizens still thot someone was "seeing things."

John Landoll, who lives near the city limits, went into his garden to quiet his dog last night. The dog had scented something. Landoll saw the shape of what appeared to be a man.

As the shape lumbered away in true anthropoid fashion. Landoll remembered the rumor about the ape. He didn't wait to see any more.

It was reported several weeks ago that an ape escaped from a circus at Sandusky.

The Sunday Messenger

ATHENS, OHIO, SUNDAY, JUNE 8, 1930.

Roaming Ape Still at Large Near Norwalk as Terrified Residents Stay in Homes, Awaiting Capture

Organized Search Planned Over Week-End for Beast That Is Reported Seen by Citizen and Two Parties of Tourists.

NORWALK, O., June 7.—Terrified women and anxious children who have remained behind locked doors in their homes for the past few days, today eagerly awaited the result of the organized search planned for this afternoon for an ape reported roaming the woods on the western outskirts of the city.

That section of the town spent a night of terror when a posse of 100 men and deputies failed to find any trace of the supposed beast in a hunt through the woods about midnight.

The young army of hunters carried shotguns, picks, clubs and rifles. Flashlights and lights from autos aided in the search.

The entire west side of the city was in a grip of terror today following the persistent reports that the animal was running wild.

John Landoll is the latest person to have reported seeing the beast in the garden at the rear of his home near the city limits. He said his dog had been barking at the animal for several nights and that on investigation he sighted the ape in a crouching position.

Others who have seen the anthropoid include two motorists from Detroit and another party of tourists from Mansfield.

Although Sheriff Harry D. Smith places little credence in the existence of the ape, he has offered the aid of deputies in finding the beast.

The Coshocton Tribune

MONDAY EVENING, JUNE 9, 1930.

Northern Ohioans Continue Search for Escaped Ape

NORWALK, O., June 9—After a week-end of intensive search residents of Huron co. were as much baffled as ever today regarding the the mysterious anthropoid that has been reported seen near the John Landoll farm, west of here.

The animal, if it is not an optical illusion or a hallucination of some sort, still remains at large. John Landoll reported seeing the animal in his garden about a week ago. He declared it resembled a huge ape.

Carl Landoll, 17, son of John Landoll. reported today that he has discovered tracks, apparently those of an ape. in the bed of Huron river near his home.

Hundreds of persons joined in a search for the mysterious creature yesterday, but no trace of the animal was found. Authorities pointed out that because of the density of the wooded region about the Landoll farm that an ape could easily elude its hunters.

THE CHRONICLE-TELEGRAM

ELYRIA, OHIO, MONDAY, JUNE 9, 1930

LOSE TRACK OF NORWALK APE

NORWALK, O., June 9 — Search for a huge ape, believed to be at large near here, was still in progress today though no one had reported seeing the animal since last week.

Carl Landoll, young farmer, discovered tracks, apparently those of the big anthropoid, in the soft mud of the Huron River Valley, to the rear of his home on the old Water Works property a short distance west of the city.

Landoll's father and several other persons reported seeing the animal in that vicinity last week. The valleys of the East Branch of Huron River and Cole Creek are as densely wooded as an African jungle and persons familiar with the country say the apo might have escape there indefinitely.

The city has been greatly interested in the search for the animal which, it is believed, might have escaped from a circus. Hundreds of Sunday motorists visited the sections where the ape was reported seen but no trace of it was found.

Carl Landoll reported that a decayed stump near his home has been torn to pieces. He believes the ape may have dug into it while searching for insects.

The more skeptical are still included to doubt that there actually is an ape at large.

The Coshocton Tribune

THURSDAY EVENING, JUNE 12, 1930.

Ohio's Ape Is Again Seen in Fremont Vicinity

FREMONT, June 12.—Interest in the "ape mystery," which has crippled this county for the past week, was heightened today when Frank Binder, of Rice tp., near here, reported that he saw the prowling anthropoid.

Posses of farmers and deputies from the county sheriff's office organized immediately and started an intensive search in the district. It was believed the animal is in thickets several miles north of this city.

Binder described the beast as a large gray animal. He declared that he chased it for some distance thru a corn field but finally lost trace of it. The animal had a "peculiar style of running," Binder said.

The strange animal was first reported seen on the western outskirts of Norwalk. A group of tourists from Detroit told city authorities they saw an ape. A motorist from Mansfield made the next report which was followed by numberous stories from truck drivers and tourists.

A thoro search by a large posse last week-end failed to reveal any trace of an ape.

SUNDAY TIMES-SIGNAL

ZANESVILLE, O., SUNDAY, JUNE 29, 1930

APE FROM CIRCUS KEEPS VILLAGERS AT HOME AT NIGHT

Residents of Ohio Town Terror Stricken; Posse to Search For Prowler

Lima, June 28—(AP)—Panic stricken residents of the village of Alger, 15 miles east of here, formed posses today to search for an ape, supposed to have escaped from a circus at Carey, O.

The animal first appeared in Alger Thursday. Mayor Lyman Clark met it on the edge of a grove, and later it was seen on the porch of the Cooney farm house. Members of the family, thinking their dog might drive the ape away, attempted to coax the dog out of the house, but the animal refused to leave. On Friday the ape appeared in a corn field where Myron Betrick was at work. He fired several shots at it from a shot gun, but the ape escaped into a woods.

For two nights Alger has appeared as a city of the dead—for there are no street lights, and residents have feared to leave their homes after dark.

Chapter Eleven
Other Bigfoot Evidence

Possible Bigfoot bedding Hamilton county

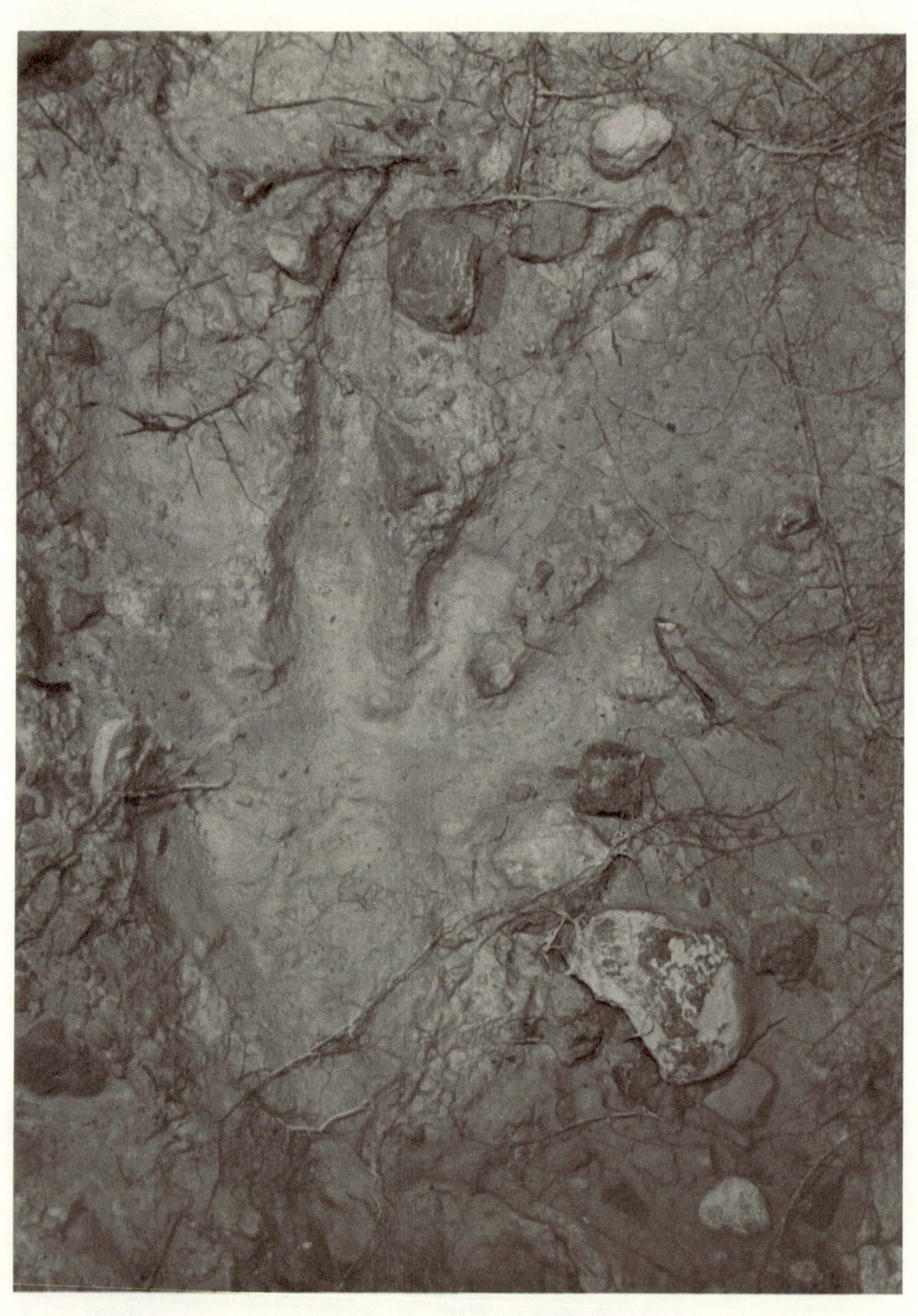

Hand print Adams County

Possible Shelter

Eyewitness sighting of a Bigfoot in a Cemetery in Hamilton county. : G Bertling was walking in a Cemetery to take pictures of the head stones when she seen what looked like a Bigfoot digging in the grown.

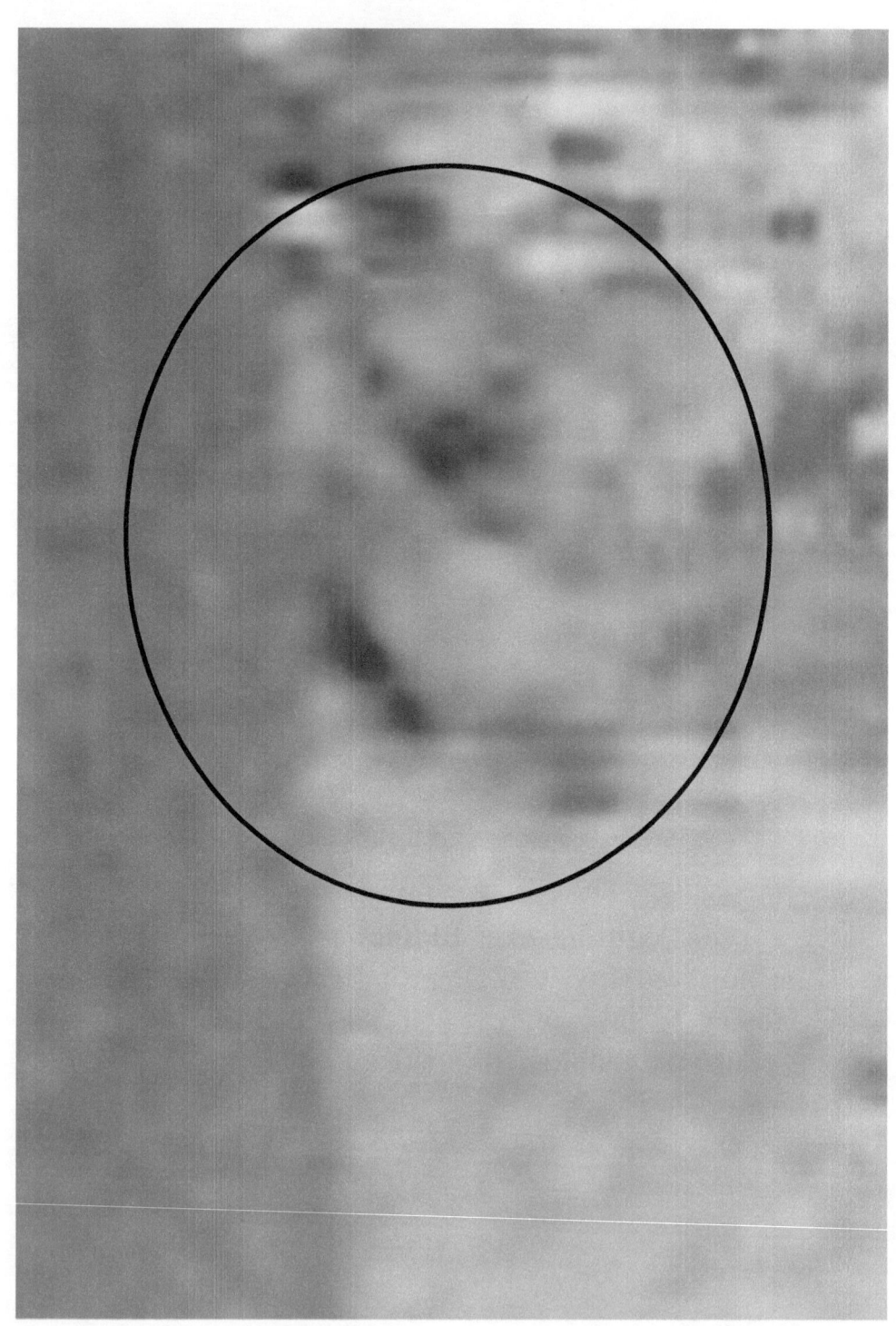

Salt Fork State Park Pictures taken by Nancy Snodgrass

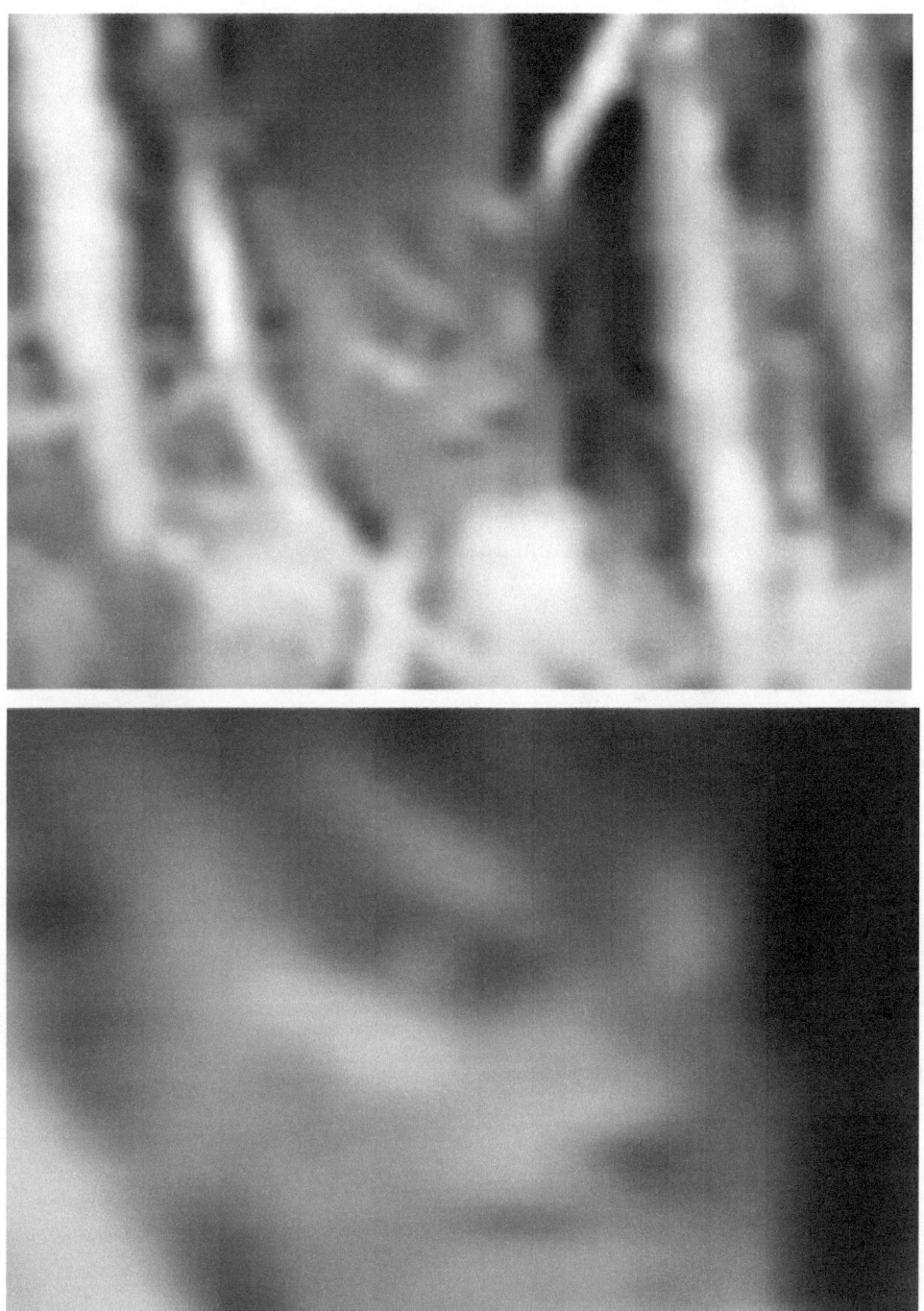

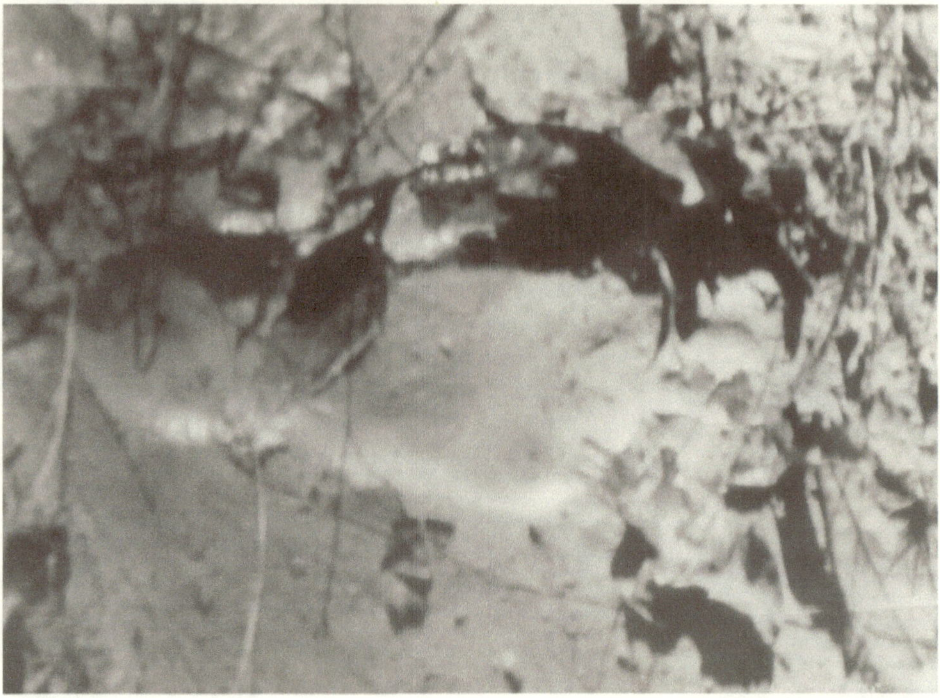

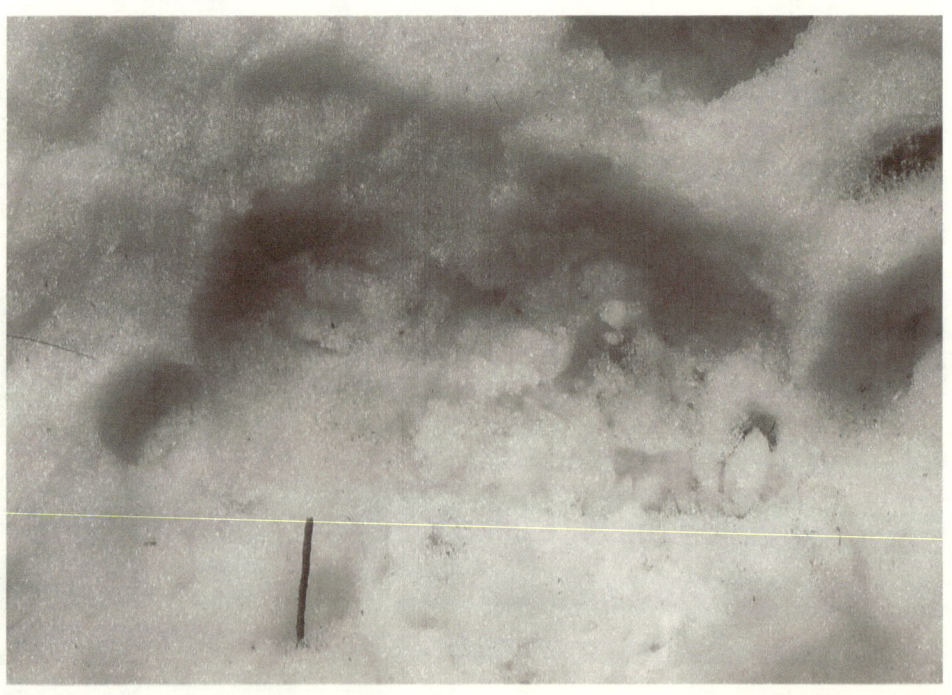

Tracks found at Salt Fork state park by Joedy Cook

NOTES

Cincinnati, Oh

NOTES

OHIO CENTER FOR BIGFOOT STUDIES

Cincinnati, Oh

www.ingramcontent.com/pod-product-compliance
Lightning Source LLC
Chambersburg PA
CBHW020513290526
45786CB00002B/581